OCR
Classical Civilisation
Reader for GCSE

Sally Knights
James Renshaw
Paul Buckley

OXFORD
UNIVERSITY PRESS

Great Clarendon Street, Oxford OX2 6DP

Oxford University Press is a department of the University of Oxford.

It furthers the University's objective of excellence in research, scholarship, and education by publishing worldwide in

Oxford   New York
Auckland   Cape Town   Dar es Salaam   Hong Kong   Karachi
Kuala Lumpur   Madrid   Melbourne   Mexico City   Nairobi
New Delhi   Shanghai   Taipei   Toronto

With offices in

Argentina   Austria   Brazil   Chile   Czech Republic
France   Greece   Guatemala   Hungary   Italy   Japan
South Korea   Poland   Portugal   Singapore   Switzerland
Thailand   Turkey   Ukraine   Vietnam

Oxford is a registered trade mark of Oxford University Press in the UK and in certain other countries

© Oxford University Press 2009

The moral rights of the author have been asserted

Database right Oxford University Press (maker)

First published 2009

All rights reserved. No part of this publication may be reproduced, stored in a retrieval system, or transmitted, in any form or by any means, without the prior permission in writing of Oxford University Press, or as expressly permitted by law, or under terms agreed with the appropriate reprographics rights organization. Enquiries concerning reproduction outside the scope of the above should be sent to the Rights Department, Oxford University Press, at the address above

You must not circulate this book in any other binding or cover and you must impose this same condition on any acquirer

British Library Cataloguing in Publication Data

Data available

ISBN 978 019 832597 0

10 9 8 7

Printed in Singapore by KHL Printing Co. Pte Ltd.

Paper used in the production of this book is a natural, recyclable product made from wood grown in sustainable forests. The manufacturing process conforms to the environmental regulations of the country of origin.

Acknowledgements
The publisher wishes to thank Nick Buckingham and Charlotte Wilshaw Kershaw for commenting on the manuscript.

Photographs: Cover photo: Bibliothèque Nationale de France; **p23** The London Art Archive/Alamy; **p41** Barbara F. McManus; **p43** Alessio Ponti/Shutterstock; **p50** The Trustees of the British Museum; **p59** Frederic Leighton/Atrrenewal center; **p61** The Trustees of the British Museum; **p62** The Trustees of the British Museum; **p69** The Trustees of the British Museum; **p72** 2000, Photo Scala, Florence - courtesy of the Ministero Beni e Att. Culturali; **p74** Walker Art Gallery, National Museums Liverpool/The Bridgeman Art Library; **p76** Supri Supri/Reuters; **p99** Ilias/hellenic-art; **p103** The Trustees of the British Museum; **p127** Vanni Archive/Corbis; **p136** Photo RMN - Les Frores Chuzeville; **p145** The Trustees of the British Museum; **p149** The Trustees of the British Museum; **p158** Barbara F. McManus; **p159** Museum of London; **p168** jthork/Fotolia.

Illustrations: pp12, 36, 47, 97 Peter Connolly; pp20, 28, 89, 109, 112, 113, 119 Peter Harper; **p117** KJA-artists.com.

Extracts from the following texts are reproduced by permission of Penguin Books Ltd.

Homer: *The Odyssey* translated by E V Rieu and revised by D C H Rieu (Penguin Classics, 1946, revised edition, 1991), copyright © 1946 by E V Rieu, this revised translation copyright © the Estate of the late E V Rieu and D C H Rieu 1991.

Ovid: *Metamorphoses* translated by David Raeburn (Penguin Books, 2004), translation copyright © David Raeburn 2004.

The audio recordings are by David Oakes with studio production by Daniel Calvert.

Contents

OCR Specification Excerpt	4
Introduction	7
Section 1 – Externally Assessed Units	**11**
1.1 Athens	12
1.2 Rome	32
1.3 Homer, *The Odyssey*	50
1.4 Ovid, *Metamorphoses*	67
1.5 Sparta	88
1.6 Pompeii	105
1.7 Tackling the written examination	122
Section 2 – Controlled Assessment Unit	**135**
2.1 Sophocles, *Antigone*	136
2.2 Aristophanes, *Lysistrata*	142
2.3 The Olympic Games	148
2.4 Virgil, *The Aeneid*	153
2.5 Pliny, *Letters*	159
2.6 Roman Britain	165
2.7 Preparing for the controlled assessment	170
Further Reading	175

OCR Specification Excerpt

GCSE Scheme of Assessment

- GCSE Classical Civilisation J280
- GCSE Classical Civilisation (Short Course) J080

For the GCSE candidates must take all **four** units.
For the GCSE (Short Course) candidates must take Unit A354 and any **one** other unit.

Unit A351 City Life in the Classical World

25% of the total GCSE marks (50% of the total GCSE Short Course marks)
1 hr written paper (60 marks)

This unit has **two** options: candidates answer questions from **one** option only. Each option has **two** sections:
Section A (Foundation Tier): Candidates are required to answer **all** questions.
Section A (Higher Tier): Candidates are required to answer **two** questions from a choice of **three**. Candidates must answer **all** the sub-questions set.
Section B (Foundation Tier): Candidates are required to answer **two** questions from a choice of **three**. Candidates must answer **all** the sub-questions set.
Section B (Higher Tier): Candidates are required to answer **one** essay question from a choice of **two**.
All assessment objectives are assessed in this unit. The unit is externally assessed.

Unit A352 Epic and Myth

25% of the total GCSE marks (50% of the total GCSE Short Course marks)
1 hr written paper (60 marks)

This unit has **two** options: candidates answer questions from **one** option only. Each option has **two** sections:
Section A (Foundation Tier): Candidates are required to answer **all** questions.
Section A (Higher Tier): Candidates are required to answer **two** questions from a choice of **three**. Candidates must answer **all** the sub-questions set.

Section B (Foundation Tier): Candidates are required to answer **two** questions from a choice of **three**. Candidates must answer **all** the sub-questions set.
Section B (Higher Tier): Candidates are required to answer **one** essay question from a choice of **two**.
All assessment objectives are assessed in this unit. The unit is externally assessed.

Unit A353 Community Life in the Classical World

25% of the total GCSE marks (50% of the total GCSE Short Course marks)
1 hr written paper (60 marks)

This unit has **two** options: candidates answer questions from **one** option only. Each option has **two** sections:
Section A (Foundation Tier): Candidates are required to answer **all** questions.
Section A (Higher Tier): Candidates are required to answer **two** questions from a choice of **three**. Candidates must answer **all** the sub-questions set.
Section B (Foundation Tier): Candidates are required to answer **two** questions from a choice of **three**. Candidates must answer **all** the sub-questions set.
Section B (Higher Tier): Candidates are required to answer **one** essay question from a choice of **two**.
All assessment objectives are assessed in this unit. The unit is externally assessed.

Unit A354 Culture and Society in the Classical World

25% of the total GCSE marks (50% of the total GCSE Short Course marks)
1 hr written paper (60 marks)

There are **six** options for controlled assessment. There will be **two** tasks set on **each** option. Candidates complete **one** task under controlled conditions.

- Each task will require candidates to analyse and evaluate original sources in order to investigate a particular aspect of the civilisation studied in each option.
- Each question will relate to one of the themes specified for the option on which it is set.

All assessment objectives are assessed in this unit. The unit is internally assessed.

OCR Specification Excerpt

Assessment Objectives

Candidates are expected to demonstrate the following in the context of the content described:

- **AO1 Knowledge** – recall, select and organise relevant knowledge of literature and its contexts and/or of society and values of the classical world;
- **AO2 Understanding** – demonstrate an understanding of literature and its contexts and/or of society and values of the classical world;
- **AO3 Interpretation and evaluation** – interpret, evaluate and respond to literature and its contexts and/or sources related to society and values of the classical world.

Introduction

Why Classical Civilisation?

It is not surprising that Classical Civilisation has become such a popular subject with students in many schools. There are very few subjects which can offer you the variety and interest that the study of the ancient world offers. You can be enthralled by the sudden and dramatic destruction of Pompeii, a city sealed in time which slowly revealed its secrets; or amazed at the military society of Sparta, its values and the roles of its women and slaves. You are free to delve into the world of ancient Athens; to see the religion and family life in the city where what was seen as democracy was born. The study of life in ancient Rome presents you with the controversy and bloodlust of the gladiators, the thrill of the chariot races and the sombre process of a Roman sacrifice.

Added to this, the literature provides a new dimension, with stories from the heroic age being the big favourites.

All the above represent a brief insight into why you can find much to enjoy and to challenge you in your study of Classical Civilisation. No greater proof is needed than the interest shown by the media in the ancient world. Numerous historical novels and films such as *Troy*, *The Three Hundred*, *The Odyssey*, *Alexander the Great* and *Augustus*, to name but a few, along with the series, *Rome*, all testify to an attraction that the ancient world brings to those who involve themselves in it.

GCSE in Classical Civilisation

Having said all of that, however, you have opted to study Classical Civilisation in the hope of gaining the best grade you can by studying a subject you enjoy. There are two main parts to the GCSE in Classical Civilisation: the written exam and the controlled assessment.

Written exam

There are three different types of question: multiple choice questions (for foundation tier candidates), essay questions (for higher tier candidates) and questions on sources (for all candidates).

Introduction

If you are entering for foundation tier then you will be asked a series of multiple choice questions. There are a number of examples of these later in the book. The chapters dedicated to the different options in Section 1 will give you a clear picture of what you need to know and ways in which you might like to approach the information.

If you are entering for higher tier then you will be asked to write an essay. Whilst the relevant chapters of the book will give you a good deal of the information you may want to use in your essays, there is also some very important advice on technique and how to approach this type of question.

Whichever tier you enter for, you will be asked to interpret ancient source material – pictures or quotes from authors or the texts you read. As well as having a number of sources in the book, you will be able to use the information from the relevant chapters here as a spur to find some of your own material and get used to comparing it. That way you will be more than prepared to do the same in the written examination.

Controlled assessment

You will also have an extended essay title to work on. You will do the research for this, bring your notes to a supervised session and write up your work with the teacher present.

Your teacher will be asked to mark your work according to the criteria which you will read about later.

The relevant chapters in Section 2 of this book will give you an outline of the topics which can be researched and how to approach them, but this is really a piece of work that relies on your commitment. Get ahead and don't leave things too late.

Approaching sources

The source material that you will be asked to respond to will take the form of either pictures of artefacts, buildings or artists' work produced in ancient times, or sometimes reconstructions of original source material. The written sources may have been produced by ancient historians, philosophers, letter writers or even playwrights.

Introduction

All the information which we have about life in the ancient world comes from sources which were produced during or immediately following those times. Sometimes the only source that we have is a later writer's view of the original source.

Just as historians and archaeologists have had to make sense of those sources in order to give a picture of life in the ancient world, you will also be asked to look at sources and, based on what you have learned about a particular topic, draw some sensible conclusions about what the source shows or illustrates.

You should not expect to know the source or have studied it. It may be completely new to you (archaeologists working in Pompeii and on other sites are finding new evidence all the time), but you will be able to identify what it shows from what you have studied. Some students in the past have panicked at the sight of an unfamiliar source. There is no need to do so. During your studies look at as many different sources as possible – even before you have read your notes – and see what you can learn from them without a text book. Ask yourself: Do all sources agree? Do they highlight the same things? Do you find out more by looking at two sources or do they contradict each other? The most important thing to remember is that when entering the examination room you should be ready and practised in the art of looking at sources objectively and taking what you can from them. Your teachers will help with this in all kinds of ways and you will be finding your own sources when you do research for your controlled assessment.

Understanding ancient society

You will be asked on a number of occasions to show understanding/evaluation of the societies that you study.

Many of the practices of the ancients seem strange and even barbaric to us, but you must try to look at them in the context of the society in which the people lived. It is of little use (and simply won't score marks) if, when asked about the importance of a Roman or Greek sacrifice, you talk about animal rights and ignore the role that sacrifice played in ancient society. Again, in terms of the role of slaves, accept that slavery existed in those times. It was pretty much the norm and condemning the Graeco-Roman world on its human rights record does not show understanding of that society.

Introduction

This does not mean that modern opinions/values do not count. Sometimes they may be relevant to your discussion of various aspects of an option. Although you will not be asked specifically for modern comparisons on the examination paper, such comparisons may form part of the controlled assessment task as you may well be asked to compare the ancient world to modern equivalents. That's the time to bring in those 21st-century values.

SECTION ONE

EXTERNALLY ASSESSED UNITS

1.1 Athens

Athens in the 5th and 4th centuries BC was one of the most vibrant and creative societies known in all human history. During these years, the city invented democracy and drama, while it was also the home of some of the greatest artists, philosophers and playwrights in European history. In fact, many of the ideas which we associate with 'western civilisation' can be traced back to classical Athens. So what made this society so remarkable?

Life at home

Houses

An Athenian house was generally modest in comparison to the grand public buildings in the city. Much of a man's life was lived out of doors, and so he was not overly concerned about what his house looked like. Houses were built on stone foundations, walls were constructed in clay bricks, while roofs were covered with clay tiles. Floors were either just beaten earth or covered with tiles or stones. Houses were rectangular and built around a central courtyard; there were not many windows in a typical house, and so this courtyard was an important source of air and light.

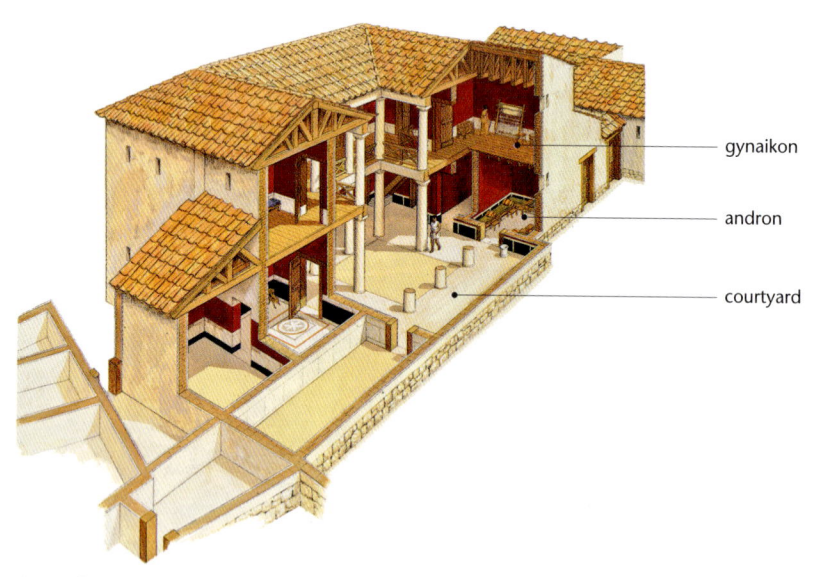

An Athenian house.

The courtyard was an important focal point for women, who were allowed out of the house only under supervision by a man. In the courtyard they could enjoy the open air and get on with household tasks such as cooking (since many houses just used portable stoves). The courtyard may also have contained a cistern to store rainwater. The main rooms of the house were focused around the courtyard; the most important room was the **andron**, or 'men's room', which was usually located near the front door. As its name suggests, the women of the family were banned from entering the **andron**. It was used as a room for the man of the house to entertain his guests. It was the only room in the house with any sort of elaborate decoration – the floor was raised on all four sides and in the centre was a pebble mosaic. Couches were placed on the elevated sides of the floor.

The other rooms of the house were less glamorous. Either at the back of the house or upstairs (if there was a second storey) was the **gynaikon**, the 'women's area'. The most important element here was the loom, since women were expected to manufacture all the cloth required for the household. The other rooms in the house might be bedrooms for children and slaves, as well as storerooms, where produce was stored for the winter months. Decoration in the house was sparing, apart from the **andron**. Most rooms were plastered and painted simply in red or white.

Kyrios and kyria

The two most important people in the household were the husband and wife, known respectively as the **kyrios** and **kyria**. The two had different but vital roles in the running of the household.

The **kyrios** was responsible first and foremost for earning money and keeping the family fed. He might well have a small farm outside the city; he would oversee its cultivation and supervise any slaves he had working for him. Some men engaged in trades in the city, such as carpentry or pottery. Beyond this, the **kyrios** was responsible for promoting the image of his family in public life, either speaking in the Assembly, making contacts in the gymnasium or hosting a good dinner party (see below). The **kyrios** had full responsibility for all members of his household, including his wife. He also owned all the property of the household, including his slaves. He had final say on matters such as whether to let a new-born child live, or whom his daughter should marry.

Externally Assessed Units

By contrast, the **kyria** had far fewer rights. She was not allowed to own any property and could only handle enough money to feed the family for a week. She had to accept every decision which her husband made and had no political rights in the city. When she was married, her father paid a dowry (a significant sum of money) to her husband. If he should divorce her, then the husband had to repay the dowry, although this went not to his ex-wife but back to her father. Women were also discouraged from going out in public; if they had to do so, then they were forced to cover up and had to be escorted by a male relative. Therefore, much of a woman's life took place inside the walls of the house.

Despite this, the **kyria** played a vital role in the success of the household. Every Athenian house tried to produce as many of its own resources as possible and the **kyria** was in charge of making sure that the slaves got on with their tasks. The most important resource produced at home was clothing, so that much of a woman's life was spent overseeing and taking part in the spinning and weaving in the **gynaikon**. She was also in charge of managing the storerooms and ensuring that the family had enough food to live off in the cold winter months. Of course, one vital responsibility for an Athenian woman was to produce healthy children – preferably sons, who could grow up to inherit the family estate in the future.

The symposium

The only time when a **kyrios** would invite guests to his house was when he was hosting a symposium – an elaborate dinner party. It was very important for a **kyrios** to carry this off well; a symposium was a good time to make political, commercial or social connections. If he gave a good impression, then he was more likely to benefit in various ways; for example, his business might benefit, or he might find a suitable marriage match for his son or daughter.

For this reason, careful preparation was required. A **kyrios** would have his slaves deliver smart invitations, he would want to offer fine food and the best wine (if he could afford to do so), and he also needed to secure the services of different types of entertainers. Our sources speak of different types of entertainment; some was innocent, such as jugglers, acrobats, mimers, musicians and dancers; however, often a key constituent of a symposium was the presence of **hetairai** – high class prostitutes.

1.1 Athens

On the day itself, guests would be greeted at the door by a slave and led into the **andron**, from which all the women of the house were barred besides slave-girls. The guests then sat on the couches around the sides of the **andron** and first had dinner. It was only after dinner that the drinking of wine took place, which was done in a very formal manner. One member of the party was responsible for supervising the sharing out of wine, the toasts, and the frequency of the rounds. It was also at this stage that the entertainers were introduced.

The guests could sometimes choose to entertain themselves. There were well-known drinking songs sung at these occasions, while a game called **kottabos** was also very popular. It involved guests flicking the remnants of drink in their cups at a target, which might be a bowl or a disc balanced on a stand. A further form of entertainment was of a far more intellectual sort – for sometimes guests chose to spend the dinner party discussing philosophy. The most famous example of this is Plato's account of a symposium, in which the philosopher Socrates leads a discussion with the other guests about the nature and varieties of love.

Slaves

Slavery was a fact of life in ancient Greece, as it has been in almost all societies until the last two hundred years or so. In Athens, perhaps as much as a third of the population was enslaved, although the Athenians generally treated their slaves well in comparison with other societies of that time.

So how did people become slaves? Some were born as children of slaves, some were captives in war, some were captured and sold by pirates, while the historian Herodotus even tells of some peoples (such as the Thracians) who sold their children into slavery for profit. In Athens, there was a slave market in the city-centre where slaves were bought and sold – it was the **kyrios'** duty to buy slaves for his family. Clearly, the value of a slave depended on his or her skills. A well-educated slave who could act as a **paidagogos** to children would probably have been highly valued. Female slaves who could sing and dance well would also be sought after as entertainers for symposiums. On the other hand, older slaves who were less strong and likely to die sooner would probably fetch a smaller price. If slaves had a particular skill, such as cobbling, metal-working or even accounting, then they could be bought and then hired out for profit by their masters. The average price for a slave seems to have been about 165 drachmas – about half a year's wages for a skilled worker.

Externally Assessed Units

There were a whole variety of roles which a slave could perform. Domestic slaves would help the **kyria** around the house; females would spin, weave or cook, while male slaves might be used to go shopping, fetch water or supervise the children's education. Stronger male slaves might be used on the family farm. Slaves skilled in a craft might be allowed to work in a workshop and sell their products, passing on part of the profits to their master. Some slaves were even bought by the state of Athens to work in the police force! Perhaps the worst life was for those slaves who were hired out to the managers of the silver mines near Athens. Conditions were dark and dangerous and many slaves died working in these conditions.

Unlike the later Roman Empire, it was not common for slaves to be freed. However, they did have some legal protection and could complain to a court if they thought that their master was treating them too badly. Despite this, many slaves no doubt had to endure harsh and humiliating conditions throughout their lives.

1. What are the similarities and differences between Athenian houses and your home?
2. How do families entertain at home today? Is there anything like a symposium in our society?
3. Do you think it was possible for any slaves in Athens to have some quality of life?

Education

Athens did not have a state education system as modern societies do today. Instead, it was the parents' decision whether a child would go to school or not. One thing is for certain – young girls were never sent to school, as it was not seen as necessary to educate them. Rather, they had to stay at home and learn the skills they would require in adult life – spinning, weaving and how to manage a household. A boy would also learn a good deal from his father about how to be a good **kyrios** in adult life; if his father was a craftsman, then the son would probably also learn his father's craft.

However, Athens did also offer a form of education for boys. There were no 'schools' as we would know them; rather, one teacher would hire out a room and teach the required subjects from there. He probably had boys of different ages and abilities in the same room. The first teacher a boy would go to would be the **grammatistes**. He would teach reading, writing and some basic arithmetic. Records suggest that the method of teaching was very repetitive, with boys having to copy down and learn by heart the works of famous poets, particularly Homer.

A few years later, a boy would start lessons with the **kitharistes**, the music teacher. Music was central to life in Athens, and it was believed that any man who could not play a musical instrument or sing was not properly educated. The **kitharistes** would teach boys to play the lyre and to sing the poems of Homer which they had already learnt with the **grammatistes**. The third part of a boy's education was physical education. Athenians believed that physical fitness was very important, not least because it prepared men for war – every Athenian citizen was expected to serve in the army. Physical education was overseen by the **paidotribes**, a PE teacher, who usually taught in a special exercise centre, the **palaistra**. Boys might learn to run, wrestle, jump or even throw a discus.

A boy's studies would be supervised by an educated family slave known as a **paidagogos**. He would accompany the boy to school, carrying his bags and sitting with him in lessons. At home, he might help with homework and would regularly update the boy's father on his progress.

> **How does Athenian education compare to the education you receive today?**

The Olympian gods

Worshipping the gods was important to Athenians at every level of their society – be it in a public festival involving the whole city, at a household level involving the whole family, or simply as a private individual. The Greeks worshipped many gods, but there were twelve who held most importance. These twelve were believed to live on Mt Olympus in northern Greece and so were known as the twelve Olympians; they were all members of the same family. Each god was responsible for a number of different areas of human life.

Externally Assessed Units

God	Role/responsibility	Symbols/portrayal
Zeus	King of the gods. Responsible for: the weather (particularly thunder and lightning), justice and the protection of foreign travellers were especially important.	Often portrayed in art either holding a thunderbolt, or sitting on a throne with a crown and sceptre (a staff indicating royal authority).
Hera	Queen of the gods and wife of Zeus, particularly important for women as the goddess of marriage. However, her own marriage was troubled, as Zeus had numerous affairs.	Like Zeus, she is often portrayed as a royal figure, wearing a crown.
Demeter	Goddess of the crops, a crucial role in an agricultural society such as ancient Greece. The most famous story about her involves the abduction of her daughter **Persephone** by Hades, the god of the Underworld.	Often pictured alongside flowers, fruit or grain.
Poseidon	God of the sea, another vital role in ancient Greece, where the people were surrounded by the seas and often made difficult voyages. He was also the god of horses.	Depicted alongside dolphins holding his trident, a three-pronged staff with which he shook the earth to create an earthquake.
Hephaistos	The god of metal-working and fire. He was lame and had an unhappy marriage to Aphrodite.	He was believed to live in volcanoes and is often portrayed around the weapons or jewellery which he had made.
Apollo	Oversaw music, the arts, education, medicine and disease, prophecy, archery and the sun. Also known as **Phoebus** ('shining').	Portrayed as a handsome young man holding a quiver of arrows or a lyre.

1.1 Athens

God	Role/responsibility	Symbols/portrayal
Artemis	The twin sister of Apollo and therefore responsible for the moon; she was often known as '**Phoebe**', the feminine form of '**Phoebus**'. She was also the goddess of hunting, childhood and childbirth.	Usually depicted with a bow and arrows with wild animals beside her.
Athene	A very important goddess for the Athenians, who believed that she had founded and given her name to their city. She was responsible for tactical warfare and wisdom, as well as weaving and handicrafts.	Her sacred bird was the owl, and she was typically portrayed in armour with weapons. She had a special cape, the **aegis**, which was made of goat-skin, fringed with images of snakes and had a picture of a gorgon's head in its centre.
Aphrodite	The goddess of love. Her son **Eros** fired arrows into people's hearts to make them fall in love.	Often portrayed with a sea-shell, since she was supposed to have been born from the sea off Cyprus, her sacred island. She is also sometimes seen with her son **Eros**.
Ares	The god of war and destruction. Military leaders would pray to Ares for help before a battle.	Portrayed wearing full armour.
Hermes	The messenger of the gods who protected the traders who travelled widely across the Greek world.	Depicted with winged sandals, a winged helmet and a special wand.
Dionysos	Responsible for wine, theatre, wild partying, as well as growth and fertility. Often accompanied by the **maenads** and **satyrs**. The **maenads** were a group of female followers who sang and danced in praise of the god. The **satyrs** were mythological creatures, half-man, half-animal, with bushy tails, snub noses, pointed ears and large phalluses.	Often shown with vines and ivy, symbols of wine and growth, as well as with the **maenads** and the **satyrs**.

Externally Assessed Units

> **TAKING IT FURTHER**
>
> Find out about the story of Demeter and Persephone. How did the Greeks use this story to explain the origins of the seasons of winter and summer?

1. Which gods would you have most wanted to worship and why?
2. Do you think it was confusing for the Athenians to have so many gods?

Worshipping the gods

Temples

The gods were usually worshipped at temples built for them in and around the city of Athens. The Athenians didn't spend a lot of money on their private houses, but instead they poured funds into the building of great temples to honour their gods. The most famous example of this is the Parthenon, the temple to Athene on top of the Acropolis in the centre of Athens.

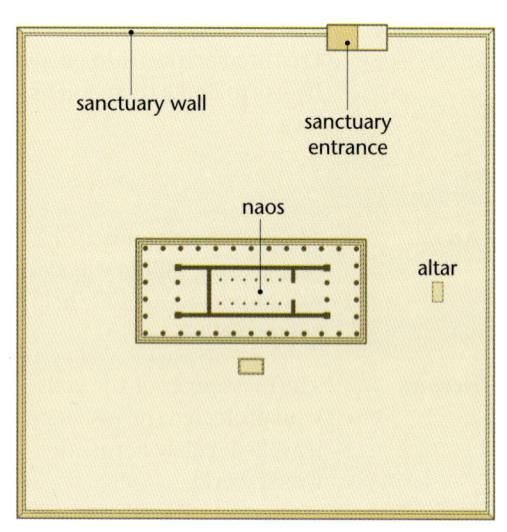

Plan of a Greek temple and sanctuary.

No religious worship actually took place in a temple. It was rather seen to be a 'home' for the god or goddess. To symbolise this, a 'cult statue' of the divinity was housed in the main room of the temple, the **naos**. Some cult statues were enormous. The statue of Athene in the Parthenon was made of gold and ivory and stood at about 12 metres in height. The main reason a worshipper might enter the temple would be to look at the statue.

All the worship took place outside the temple. Every temple was part of a religious sanctuary which was marked off by a wall. The whole of the sanctuary was considered to be 'holy ground'. The focal point in the sanctuary was the altar, where sacrifices took place. This was situated outside the front of the temple so that all the blood from the sacrificed animals would flow away into the ground.

Sacrifice

A sacrifice to a god or goddess was a way for a person either to thank that immortal for any benefits received in his life or to ask for help in the future. The whole process was carefully designed so that a person was giving a present to a god – much as we might take care to gift wrap a birthday present for a friend or relative today. Anything could be given in sacrifice – sometimes it was food such as cakes or fruit, sometimes drink in the form of milk or wine, while some even gave other items; for example, a soldier might dedicate a shield after being successful in battle.

However, the most important type of sacrifice was that of an animal. Various types of animal were used for different gods at distinct times in the year. The most common animals to sacrifice were cows, pigs, piglets, goats and sheep. The most important steps in the sacrificial procedure are outlined on page 22.

Externally Assessed Units

1. Once the **animal** had been purchased, it was prepared for sacrifice. Ribbons were put on its head and its horns were painted with gold. The animal was then led to the sanctuary for sacrifice – if it went willingly, it was seen to be a good omen.

2. All the **participants** washed themselves thoroughly in preparation for the sacrifice and put on garlands. A maiden carried a basket full of barley grain; she hid the knife inside this basket. A flute-player also played throughout the ceremony.

3. The **priest** poured water on the animal's head, causing it to nod – this was interpreted as the animal consenting to the sacrifice. The priest then said a prayer of offering, took the knife and approached the victim.

4. Another participant then **stunned** the animal by hitting the back of its head with a club. The priest then cut the animal's throat. The blood was collected in a bowl and poured on the top and the sides of the altar.

5. The **meat** from the animal was cut up and treated in three ways. The thighbones were cut off, wrapped in fat and burnt on the altar. The smoke was said to rise to the heavens and nourish the gods. The entrails (guts) of the animal were cut out and inspected for omens. The rest of the meat was then boiled and shared out among all the participants – this was one of the only times when ancient Greeks ate meat, so it was a real feast and a chance for the community to come together.

Imagine you are an Athenian who has taken part in a sacrifice. Write an account of the occasion.

The Panathenaia

One vital aspect of Athenian religion was the celebration of religious festivals. There were over 120 festival days in Athens; the most important festival was the Panathenaia, the celebration of Athene's birthday which took place at the end of July each year. In fact, every four years this festival was even grander and became known as the 'Great Panathenaia'; it lasted for about eight days and saw a whole range of sporting, musical and religious events to celebrate Athene, the patron goddess of the city.

The procession

The main event of the festival was the grand procession through the city of Athens towards the Acropolis. At the end of the procession the Athenians presented the statue of Athene on the Acropolis with a birthday present – a new robe, known as a **peplos**, which had been specially woven that year by the young women of Athens. The **peplos** was always gold and purple in colour and into its fabric were woven scenes from the mythological victory of the Olympian gods over the Giants, which symbolised the triumph of order over chaos.

The procession began at dawn at the Dipylon gate (the city's largest gate) and headed through the city to the Acropolis. At least 100 sacrificial animals were driven along the route, while the procession itself was very ordered, with many levels of Athenian society represented, including young women, priestesses of Athene, **metics** (foreigners resident in Athens), musicians, old men, soldiers

Presenting the **peplos** to Athene: a scene from the Parthenon frieze.

and horsemen. When they arrived at the Acropolis, only Athenian citizens were allowed up onto the sanctuary; here the animals were sacrificed and the **peplos** was given to the statue of Athene. Afterwards, there was a great feast of the sacrificial meat for all the city.

The Parthenon frieze

The frieze (continuous sculpted display) around the Parthenon temple on the Acropolis is believed to depict the procession at the Panathenaia. The frieze builds up to a point where a young girl hands over a robe – the **peplos** – to a man, with the Olympian gods watching on. Much of the frieze is today housed in the British Museum.

> **TAKING IT FURTHER**
>
> Find out about why so much of the Parthenon Frieze came to be housed in the British Museum. Who was Lord Elgin and what role did he play in this? What are the arguments for and against this display being returned to the Greek authorities?

Musical events

There were also various musical events at the festival, where winning competitors were rewarded with valuable prizes, including large sums of money and golden crowns. **Rhapsodes** (reciters of epic poetry) competed over retelling passages from Homer's *Iliad* and *Odyssey*, while there were also competitions for who could best play and accompany the lyre and the aulos, two Greek musical instruments similar to the modern harp and oboe respectively.

Sporting events

The sporting games at the Panathenaia were one of the most important athletic festivals in the Greek world, attracting competitors from all over Greece. Most of the events were the same as those contested at the Olympic Games (see pages 148–152), including the 200-metre sprint (**stadion**), pentathlon, wrestling, boxing and equestrian events.

1.1 Athens

In contrast to the Olympic Games, victors at the Panathenaia were rewarded with great prizes – large jars (**amphoras**) of olive oil, each of which had a picture of Athene on one side and the event in which the competitor had won on the other. Olive oil was a very valuable commodity in the ancient world, and so a charioteer who won 140 **amphoras** of olive oil was rich indeed!

Tribal contests

Since both the musical and sporting events were open to all Greeks, the Athenians produced some events which were open only to Athenian citizens, so giving a distinctly local feeling to this Athenian festival. These events were competitions between the ten tribes of the city and so were known as tribal contests. Included in these tribal contests were: a torch race from the Dipylon Gate to the Acropolis, where sprinters had to run the distance holding a torch; and boat races in a great rowing regatta at Piraeus, the harbour of Athens.

Athenian politics

The Panathenaic festival and the City Dionysia festival (see page 26 below) were also important opportunities for the Athenians to show off their city to the rest of the Greek world. Non-Athenians were invited to both festivals and would surely have been impressed by the wealth, power and religion of the largest city of the Greek world. Athenians believed that their city had become so powerful because of their democratic system, and so these public festivals were a chance for them to display their democracy and its successes in action.

The city of Athens was the first to come up with a system of democracy, a concept whereby every citizen had a vote in political decisions. However, women and slaves were not counted as citizens, so it was actually only a minority of the population who had the vote. The following were the most important aspects of the democracy:

- **The Assembly**. Every citizen was a member of the city's assembly, which voted to make new laws.

- **The Council**. 500 citizens selected by lot sat on this each year; they were effectively the city's civil service.

Externally Assessed Units

> - **The Tribes.** Each citizen was a member of one of the city's ten tribes. Each tribe had to provide a certain number of men for the council.
>
> - **The Magistrates.** There were nine **archons**, or magistrates, who served for a year and oversaw various areas of public life, including the law courts.

Which events would you have most liked to have watched or taken part in at the Panathenaia?

The City Dionysia

The second most important festival in the Athenian calendar was the City Dionysia, held in late March in honour of the god Dionysos. Since Dionysos was the god of drama, the City Dionysia was a grand drama festival; playwrights wrote plays specifically for the event, and these were then judged in order of merit. In this sense, the City Dionysia was similar to a modern film festival, such as that at Cannes, where film directors put forward their latest films for the honour of winning first prize.

Careful preparations were needed for the City Dionysia. These started in the previous summer, when one of the city's magistrates, the **archon**, had to select playwrights to write plays for the festival. He chose three tragic playwrights, who each wrote three tragedies and a satyr-play (a light-hearted parody of a tragedy), and three comic playwrights, who each wrote a single comedy. When the playwrights had written their plays, they then had to hire a cast and spend months rehearsing the plays. Each playwright was funded by a wealthy citizen known as a **choregos**, who paid for things like costumes, special effects and props; he would welcome the opportunity to try to put on the very best show possible in the hope that he would win popularity and respect from his fellow citizens.

On the night before the festival began, there was a **torchlight procession** in which a wooden statue of Dionysos was led into the city from outside the walls. It was escorted by the city's military cadets and led into the theatre, where it remained for the rest of the festival. On the first day of the festival there was another **grand procession**, in which many animals were led to the temple of Dionysos and sacrificed. The celebrations went on until late in the evening.

On the second, third and fourth days of the festival the plays were performed. Each day began early with three tragedies and a satyr-play, all from the same playwright; after lunch, one of the comic plays was put on. Before the plays began on the second day, there was a magnificent **opening ceremony** in the theatre. During this, all the money paid to Athens in tax by its allies was displayed in the theatre, while orphaned boys whose fathers had died fighting for the city paraded in. Individual citizens who had done great deeds for the city were also awarded prizes.

Judging

The Athenians developed a complicated way of judging the plays, which was very democratic. Although foreign visitors were welcome at the festival, the vast majority of the audience would have been Athenian citizens, who sat in one of ten tribal areas in the theatre. The judges were drawn from the audience as follows:

1. Before the festival, each tribe put some names of its citizens into a sealed urn.

2. At the beginning of the festival, one name was chosen at random from each of the ten urns. These ten citizens were then installed as judges.

3. On the fifth day of the festival, each judge wrote down the names of the playwrights in order of merit on a tablet (there was a different prize for tragedy and comedy). The ten tablets were then placed in an urn.

4. The **archon** drew out five of the ten tablets at random. The playwright with the most votes was declared the winner.

Externally Assessed Units

The theatre

The ancient Athenians invented drama in the western world. One part of their legacy left to us was the design of a theatre building. In Athens, the main theatre was the Theatre of Dionysos, which was built into the hillside on the south side of the Acropolis. This theatre was part of a religious sanctuary to Dionysos, showing the close connection between religion and drama. The seating area in the theatre, known as the **theatron**, was cut out of the steep slope and designed to seat more than 15,000. The rise in the seats gave every spectator a good view of the stage; moreover, Greek theatres were designed to create excellent acoustics, so that even spectators sitting in the back row could hear every sound made by the actors.

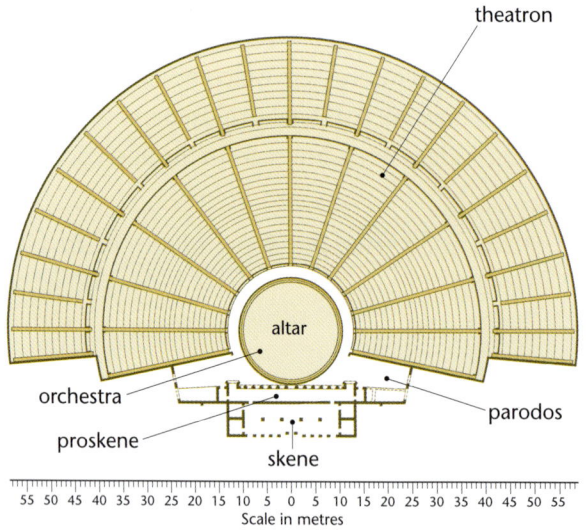

Plan of a Greek theatre.

The acting area itself was divided into different parts (see plan). The **orchestra** was where the chorus (see below) sang and acted. In the middle of this area was an altar to Dionysos, where sacrifices to the god were held every morning before the plays began. On either side of the orchestra were the **parodoi**, entrance pathways by which both the chorus and the audience entered the theatre. To the back of the **orchestra** was the raised stage, which was known as the **proskene**, behind which was a wooden building known as the **skene**. Actors would change inside this building, and it was also a place for the storing of props. In the front of the **skene** there was a set of central double-doors, which usually represented the entrance into a building.

When we go to the theatre today, we are used to various special effects such as amplified sound, dry ice, and spotlights. However, the Athenian theatre had very little by way of special effects and so the quality of the acting had to be very high for the play to be a success. Despite this, there were one or two devices which were used to add to the experience. As you can see in the plan, to the right of the **skene** there was a crane-like device, the **mekhane**, which could hoist actors into the air. Usually an actor on the **mekhane** was playing a god, and so giving the impression of coming down to the earth from the heavens. Also in the plan is the **ekkuklema**, a trolley-like device which was rolled through the double-doors, usually with a dead body on it. This scene was taken to represent what had happened inside the house – usually the murder of an important character.

The plan also shows the three levels where actors could act. The chorus would always remain in the **orchestra**, while the main actors would act on the **proskene** or climb up onto the roof of the **skene** – again this area was usually reserved for gods to allow them to appear above the level of human beings. Further atmosphere was added to the set by the painting of the front of the **skene**, which usually represented a building such as a temple or palace. A final device which could add to a play was the thunder-machine – this apparently involved the rolling of rocks underneath seats to create the sound of thunder.

Tragedy and comedy

Two different types of play developed in Athens. A tragedy was a very serious and grand play which asked some of life's deepest questions, such as why people suffer, or how much the gods look after human beings. The main character of a tragedy was usually a hero who suffered a major catastrophe and had to cope with it as bravely as possible. There were no happy endings in tragedy.

By contrast, a comedy was a riotous and hilarious experience! Comedies were usually set in everyday Athens and made fun of the city's people, particularly its politicians and well-known public figures, such as the general Cleon or the philosopher Socrates. There was lots of bawdy behaviour and rude jokes in comedies and in some ways they are best compared to a modern pantomime.

The three actors

One important rule of Athenian theatre was that each play could only have three main actors. However, that is not to say that there were only three characters in a play. Rather, the three actors had to play a range of parts in a play, perhaps as many as five distinct character roles. To enable them to carry this off, actors wore masks which covered the whole head. These masks, which were made of linen, cork or wood, normally with some hair at the top, allowed them to appear in a variety of roles.

Tragic masks usually had serious and thoughtful expressions suited to tragic actors. The rest of the costume of a tragic actor had a similar tone. The main item was a long robe, over which a cloak could be worn. Costumes were colourful and decorated with a patchwork of patterns, often reflecting the royal or heroic qualities of a tragic character. Actors wore soft leather boots on their feet. Tragic plays were normally set in the heroic past, and so actors would play characters such as gods, goddesses, kings or queens. Slaves and soldiers were also common roles in tragedies.

By contrast, the comic costume was designed to play for laughs. The mask itself usually looked ridiculous and over-sized; the costume, consisting of a short tunic and tights, was thickly padded, so allowing the actors to roll around in slapstick fashion. The most amusing and distinct element was the large leather phallus worn by male characters, which could be used to simulate an erection! Dionysos was the god of fertility and so the phallus was especially linked to his worship. Since comic plays were based on everyday Athenian life, they usually had 'stock characters', such as a simple country farmer, a smooth-talking city dweller, a grumpy old man or a clever slave.

The chorus

In a tragedy, there were 15 chorus members, but this number went up to 24 for a comedy. They were not professional actors but amateurs selected from the citizen body of Athens. The chorus sang and danced in the **orchestra** between scenes in a play; they were therefore a crucial part of the action. They gave the main actors time to change in the **skene**, while they also played characters in the play. They usually played townsfolk who watch the main action of the play, sometimes commenting on it, sometimes giving the audience background information, and sometimes creating a mood of tension or suspense in the build-up to a vital moment.

The chorus members usually all wore a uniform costume – a mask and clothes which indicated their status in society (e.g. old men might wear dignifed robes). In a comedy, choruses were often made up of animals. The playwright Aristophanes wrote comedies entitled *Birds*, *Frogs*, and *Wasps*, and in each play the chorus members all dressed as the respective animals – something which must have provided great amusement for the audience.

1. **Would you have preferred to have watched a tragedy or a comedy in Athens?**
2. **Do you think the system of judging the plays was a good one?**

1.2 Rome

The Roman Empire still captures the imagination today. It is the remarkable story of one city which grew over a number of centuries to become the master of lands, stretching from northern England to southern Egypt (north to south), and from Iraq to Portugal (east to west). Much of our society today is descended from the civilisation developed by the Romans, and this section will examine that civilisation and how the Romans lived in their day to day lives until the empire collapsed in the 5th century AD.

Life at home

The paterfamilias

The **paterfamilias** was the male head of a Roman household. The Roman word 'familia' meant more than our notion of 'family'; it included all the slaves and property of the house and so really meant something more like 'household'. The **paterfamilias** had legal power over the whole household. In early Roman times, this included the power of life and death, although by the time of the empire, this was only really the case for a new-born child. If a baby born into the household was unwanted or illegitimate, then the **paterfamilias** could choose to have it abandoned and left to die.

The **paterfamilias** was responsible for the welfare of his family. He would certainly want to oversee the education of his children (particularly his sons), and might appoint a slave known as a **paedagogus** to act as a tutor. He would speak regularly with the **paedagogus** about how the studies were progressing. When his daughter reached puberty, the father was responsible for arranging her marriage – very often this happened without the girl having any say at all. The **paterfamilias** would expect his wife to be loyal and hard-working in the home, while he would also have to manage the purchase of any slaves for the household.

He was also the religious head of the family. Every morning he would gather the whole household together at the family shrine, the **lararium**, where the spirits of the family's ancestors, known as **lares**, were worshipped. He would lead the family in prayers and offerings; it was only after this that the day's work could start. The **paterfamilias** was also in charge of making sure that other religious rites involving the family were held according to proper custom. These might include an offering to the spirits of the larder, the **penates**, before a meal, or offerings to the correct gods at important rites of passage such as birth, marriage and funerals.

He was also the family's breadwinner, and so would frequently be away from the house at work. If he was wealthy enough, then he might be a **patron** to some **clients**. Roman society was based around this **patron/client** relationship. Poorer Romans in need of money would attach themselves as **clients** to a wealthy man, the **patron**. **Clients** were expected to appear at their **patron's** house at dawn every morning; later, they might be required to accompany him to the forum or to the baths. In the city, they acted as their master's supporters and were expected to vote for him if he ran for political office. In return, **clients** would hope for a small hand out of money or a gift each day; if they were particularly lucky, they might even be invited to dine with their **patron** in the evening.

The wife

Women were regarded as minors in Roman law, holding the same status as children. They could not vote and had no say in the Roman political system. A woman was under the control of her **paterfamilias** throughout her life. In certain cases he retained this control even when she married; in other cases her husband rather than her father became her **paterfamilias**. However, it is hard to make one statement about how women were treated in ancient Rome. They seem to have been given more freedom as the centuries passed, while a woman's quality of life depended to a great extent on her social background and the character of her husband.

A wife was expected to spend much of her time at home, where her main role was to manage the household (that said, it was not uncommon for women to visit friends, or go to public places such as the market, the temple or the baths). She was expected to assign the slaves their various duties in the house (such as cleaning, cooking, or collecting water), and then check that these were being done properly. Another important responsibility was to manage the spinning and weaving in the house, since Roman families tried to produce as much of their own cloth as possible.

A further important role for a wife was to bring up her children. Although she probably had slaves to help her, a mother was expected to oversee the nursing

Externally Assessed Units

of infants, and then to ensure that her sons went to school and that her daughters learnt the duties required of a Roman woman. Motherhood was far more dangerous in Roman times – women had a much higher chance of suffering from infection during childbirth. If they survived this, then they might well live longer than their child. We hear of one woman who was married at 11 and died at 27; she had six children, but only one survived her.

Clearly, there was a great difference in the lifestyles of rich and poor women. Poverty might have forced some women out to work on stalls in the market or in industries such as washing and cleaning. By contrast, wealthy women could enjoy great luxury. We hear a number of accounts of rich wives whose first engagement of the day is to be dressed by their slaves – this would include fitting their clothes, having their hair done and then adding perfume, make-up and jewellery.

Slavery

Slavery was an accepted part of life in the Roman Empire, as it has been in most societies until fairly recently. The empire relied on the labour of its slaves in both public and private life, and it is fair to say that it could not have survived without them.

There were various ways in which people fell into slavery. The most common was to be captured in war; as the Roman Empire grew and conquered more peoples, it produced a steady supply of slaves. However, there were other routes into slavery. Any babies born to a slave mother automatically held slave status (even if the father was a citizen, as regularly happened), and other babies abandoned by their parents at birth might be saved and brought up as slaves. Other people were captured by pirates and sold into slavery – some parts of the Roman Empire were notoriously dangerous for travellers. Finally, some criminals could be condemned to slavery, where they would have to train as gladiators or work in the mines.

Once captured, slaves might be taken to Rome or the Greek island of Delos, both of which had large slave markets. Each slave would be forced to stand on a revolving platform at the market, with a placard hanging from his or her neck giving information about them. The slave-trader would guarantee that he owned the slaves legally and that they were in a healthy condition and not wanted for any crime. Slaves typically fetched between 500 and 2,000 **denarii**, depending on the talents they had to offer.

The quality of a slave's life was dependent on these talents. Educated Greek slaves were highly valued as tutors for children, while women were bought to help the Roman wife in domestic tasks such as childcare, cooking, weaving and shopping. Male domestic slaves would be required to work for the **paterfamilias**, perhaps doing his accounts, accompanying him to the baths or running errands. Stronger male slaves might be marked down for more challenging or dangerous tasks. Some were sent down the mines, where conditions were grim and life expectancy relatively short; others would work on one of the many large farming estates in the empire. The fittest and strongest might be sent to gladiator school.

The treatment of slaves depended not just on a slave's job but also on his master's character. A master's rights over his slaves in the period of the early empire were total – he could even have them killed – and some masters could be incredibly cruel, subjecting their slaves to frequent physical and sexual abuse. On the other hand, we also hear of some slave/master relationships which were clearly warm and trusting. Slaves had no political rights, nor could they marry or own property, although there were one or two laws giving them a degree of legal protection in the period of the later Roman Empire. They were also allowed to earn and save money, which they could later use to buy their freedom.

The freeing of slaves was a notable feature of Roman society. A master could choose to free a slave if he had served him well over a long period, performed an outstanding act, or if he had saved enough money to buy his freedom. Once free, ex-slaves had the status of 'freedmen'. A freedman would usually take his former master's family name. Some freedmen managed to go on and make a lot of money in trade and business: freedmen were among the wealthiest people in Pompeii at the time of its eruption. They were not allowed the full rights of a Roman citizen, as they could not stand for political office in Rome, but their children were given full Roman citizenship.

The dinner party

In common with many societies, Romans held dinner parties to enjoy the company of friends and to make new business or social contacts. They were held in the house's dining room, known as a **triclinium** (literally: 'three-couch room'), since it contained three couches on which guests would recline while they ate. Normally, each couch could fit three guests. The couches were covered in mattresses for comfort and each place was divided by cushions. Guests lay in the reclining position, leaning on their left elbows and taking food from the central table.

A dinner party was known as a **cena**, and typically had three courses (although we hear of parties with as many as seven!). The first course might be made up of light appetisers, such as eggs, olives, or salads; these were followed by wine sweetened by honey. The main course was typically a selection of meats or fish accompanied by vegetables and a variety of sauces. Finally came dessert, which might consist of fruit, nuts, or simple sweet-cakes.

A Roman dinner party.

After the meal was over, the party might have a session of prolonged wine drinking. Wine was always watered down heavily, and so Romans could survive the many rounds of drinks – it was customary for the host to raise a toast and then for all the guests to drain their cups in one go. As the guests drank, entertainment might also be provided. This would perhaps include slave-girls dancing or playing musical instruments, comedians performing, or gambling games such as dice. A more intellectual dinner party might include poetry recitals or philosophical discussion.

1. What are the similarities and differences between Roman families and families today?
2. Do you think it was possible for any slaves in Rome to have some quality of life?

Education

In early Roman times there were no schools as we would understand them. Children simply learnt from their parents – fathers would teach their sons their own trades, as well as some basic literacy and numeracy, while mothers would teach their daughters how to manage the household. However, as Rome grew it quickly became influenced by Greek civilisation; as a result, the Romans adopted a similar form of education as that practised in Athens (see page 16).

Schools therefore began to emerge, although they would not be easily recognisable to us today. The school building was really nothing more than a simple room hired by the teacher; it might even be the back room of a shop, with customers coming and going. Pupils sat on wooden stools and the teacher on a seat, but apart from that there was not likely to be much furniture. Teachers could not afford anything grander – there are many stories of how poorly paid they were!

It is hard to know exactly what proportion of pupils went to school. It is likely that the majority of boys attended the first stage of education, while a significant number of girls probably attended school for a time at this stage too. However, the main purpose of a girl's education was to prepare her for her duties of managing the household as a wife. The second and third stages of education were really reserved for the sons of the rich; by the age of 14, girls were getting married and boys from poorer families had started working. The very wealthiest families could even afford to have their children educated by a private tutor instead of attending school at the first stage of the education system.

The first stage of a Roman education was at the school of the **litterator**. Boys and girls would attend his lessons from the age of seven and learnt reading, writing and some basic arithmetic. The education was very repetitive at this stage – pupils had to practise writing letters endlessly and, once they had mastered the alphabet, they were forced to copy out useful phrases such as *laborare est orare* (to work is to pray). The following extract from the diary of a Roman schoolboy gives voice to a pupil's experience:

> *I copy the letters and then show the work to the teacher. He corrects it and copies it out properly. I get ready to start again by rubbing the wax smooth – that's a job, the wax is too hard. Here we go: ink and papyrus now. Up ... and down ... up and down ... and then along comes teacher and says I deserve to be whipped!*

Externally Assessed Units

The boy's words tell us a lot about the equipment used by Roman pupils. They first used wax tablets – thin sheets of wood covered with wax, on which pupils could write with a **stilus**, an implement with a sharp end for marking the wax and a flat end to rub the wax out and reset it. When pupils were competent writers, they would be allowed to move on to write with a pen and ink on a papyrus, thick reed paper invented in ancient Egypt.

The second stage of education for those whose parents could afford it started at the age of about 14. It was with a teacher known as a **grammaticus**, who taught his pupils Greek and Latin literature, which could include works of poetry, drama, history or philosophy. Virgil's *Aeneid*, which told of the escape from Troy to Italy by Aeneas (whom the Romans believed to be their ancestor), was a standard text, much like Shakespeare has been in the English speaking world. Pupils were taught to read it aloud and to comment on grammar, figures of speech (such as similes), the poet's use of mythology and other matters.

At the age of 16, these privileged children would progress to studying with the **rhetor**. He taught them the art of public speaking, a crucial skill in a world without the various means of communication which today we take for granted – newspapers, email, the internet, radio and television. A successful public figure in Rome had to be able to speak well in front of a large crowd of people. Pupils were taught to deliver their speeches with facial expression and hand gestures; they practised speaking by arguing about issues from history or literature, such as: 'Should Hannibal have invaded Italy?' or 'Should Dido have committed suicide?' The pupils' training at this stage was similar to a barrister's training today, and it is no surprise that many of Rome's most leading politicians were also accomplished lawyers.

> How does Roman education compare to the education you receive today?

State gods and goddesses

The gods were a vital part of Roman life. The Romans were heavily influenced by the Greek civilisation which had developed to the east and in the south of Italy, and so in early times they matched up their gods with the Greek equivalents (see page 18). In essence, they were the same gods but with a different name (apart from Apollo, who kept his Greek name). For this reason, the Greek name of the Roman god has been put in brackets.

God	Role/responsibility	Symbol/portrayal
Jupiter (Zeus)	King of the gods. The most powerful of all the gods and his temple was usually the most important one in a Roman town.	He was originally a weather god who controlled the skies (hence his symbol, the thunderbolt), but in his role as ruler of the gods he is also seen with a sceptre.
Neptune (Poseidon)	Jupiter's brother and the god of the sea. Also important to the Romans as the god of horses and therefore of chariot racing.	Depicted with his symbol, a trident, which he banged on the earth to create earthquakes, and sometimes also with a dolphin.
Mars (Ares)	The god of war. He was also particularly important for Romans as he was believed to be the father of Romulus, the founder of Rome.	In art, he is typically represented with armour – a shield, helmet, sword and breastplate.
Apollo (Apollo)	A god of prophecy, the arts (music, literature, art, etc), the sun and archery. Like the Greeks, the Romans also worshipped him as the god of the sun and called him **Phoebus**, which means 'shining'.	Bow and arrows, lyre, sun.
Mercury (Hermes)	The messenger of the gods; his role therefore developed to include responsibility for communications, trade and business, so that he was particularly worshipped by travellers and merchants.	His most famous symbols are his winged sandals and wand.
Pluto (Hades)	The brother of Jupiter and Neptune and king of the Underworld, where he ruled over the dead. Pluto literally means 'wealthy' because of the vast number of souls over which he ruled.	Romans did not like to depict him very often, but when they did so he is typically represented with a sceptre or a pomegranate fruit.

(Continued)

Externally Assessed Units

God	Role/responsibility	Symbol/portrayal
Juno (Hera)	The queen of the gods and the wife (and sister) of Jupiter. She was particularly important to the Romans as a goddess of women, who had responsibility for childbirth and marriage.	In art, she might be seen with a new-born child, supervising a wedding, or in regal dress wearing a crown.
Venus (Aphrodite)	The goddess of love. The Romans believed that she was the mother of the legendary Aeneas, who brought the Trojans to Italy after the Trojan war; one of his descendants was Romulus, the founder of Rome.	Often represented in art without many clothes, and in the company of her son, **Cupid (Eros)**. Her symbol was a shell because she was believed to have been born from the sea off Cyprus.
Minerva (Athena)	Important for a variety of skills, including tactical warfare and wisdom, as well as arts and crafts.	Often represented with a helmet, spear and her special cape, the aegis. Her sacred bird was the owl, which was also her symbol.
Diana (Artemis)	The twin sister of Apollo and, like Minerva, a virgin goddess. She was the goddess of hunting and of the moon (just as her brother was god of the sun).	In art, she is often represented as a huntress, with bows, arrows and a hunting dog.
Ceres (Demeter)	The goddess of the harvest (particularly grain) and of motherly love. She was particularly close to her daughter **Proserpina (Persephone)**, who was abducted and taken down to the Underworld by Pluto.	Often depicted in art with a sceptre, a basket of flowers and fruit, and a garland made of wheat ears.
Vesta (Hestia)	The Roman goddess of the hearth, which was a vital part of every Roman home since it gave warmth and light, as well as allowing people to cook. Vesta also had an important temple in the Roman forum, which symbolised the hearth of the city.	Fire.

1. Which gods would you have most wanted to worship and why?
2. Do you think it was confusing for the Romans to have so many gods?

Worshipping the gods

Temples

The design of a typical Roman temple was influenced by that of a Greek temple (see page 20). A temple was rectangular in shape, and based on a high podium. No religious worship actually took place in a temple. It was rather seen to be a 'home' for the god or goddess. To symbolise this, a 'cult statue' of the divinity was housed in the main room of the temple, the **cella**. The only reason a worshipper might enter the temple would be to admire the statue, and to leave gifts such as jewels, precious ornaments and flowers.

In front of the **cella** was an entry porch, while behind it was a storeroom for the temple's attendants. As in Greece, the temple was decorated with a variety of sculptures. Outside its front was the altar, where animals were led to sacrifice – this had to be done outside so that all the blood would flow away into the ground.

Sacrifice

The principle of a sacrifice was that a worshipper gave up something valuable to a god; in return, he hoped that the god would look kindly on him in the future. Therefore, a farmer might sacrifice to Ceres before a harvest, or a sailor might give an offering to Neptune before a sea voyage. Sacrifice did not necessarily involve the killing of an animal, but could take the form of any gift. Usually sacrifices were

Image of a sacrifice, from the Temple of Vespasian, Pompeii.

Externally Assessed Units

symbolic of life in some way – milk, cheese, fruit or cakes were often given. However, the most common type of sacrifice was the offering of an animal in a ritual killing.

A Roman preparing to make a sacrifice would first have to agree an appointed time with the priest of the relevant temple. On the appointed day, he would then go to the market to buy an animal. It would have to be perfect, without any blemish. Certain animals were normally offered to specific gods; for example, a heifer (a young female cow) was often given to Jupiter. The sacrificer would wear his best toga, tie ribbons to the animal's horns and tail, and lead it through the streets to the temple. If the animal didn't go willingly or stumbled along the way, then this was seen as a bad omen and he might want to start the whole process again with a new animal.

The ceremony took place on the altar outside a temple and was overseen by a priest, who would cover his head with the folds of his toga. He would also wash his hands in sacred water before the ceremony. The animal's head was sprinkled with wine and **mola salsa** (sacred bread baked by the Vestal Virgins), while the priest said a prayer. The animal was then stunned by a hammer blow delivered by an attendant, after which a man carrying a knife cut its throat. The animal was then disembowelled and its innards removed, which a soothsayer would examine to look for omens. If the innards were discoloured or misshapen, then he would declare bad omens. Any glitch in the entire ceremony could also be interpreted as a bad omen, and then the process would have to be begun all over again. A flute player played throughout, trying to drown out any unwanted sounds – even a sneeze could be interpreted as a bad omen.

If the omens were good, then the process continued. The innards were then burnt in a fire on the altar as an offering to the god. The rest of the meat was then cooked and shared out to the participants at a feast.

1. How does a Roman temple compare to a modern place of worship?
2. Imagine you are a Roman who has taken part in a sacrifice. Write an account of the occasion.

Amphitheatres

The Colosseum in Rome was one of the great buildings of the ancient world. However, the magnificence of the building makes it easy to forget its function; it was really a 'theatre of death', where huge crowds came to watch people suffer and die in great pain. While there is now a great deal of glamour attached to gladiators, it is important to remember the horrific pain so many suffered in this immense public torture chamber.

The Colosseum, Rome.

The Colosseum held 50,000 people and there were 80 separate entrances, allowing everyone to get in and out of their seats quickly. This was not the only efficient design in the building: if the sun was beating down too fiercely, then an enormous awning could be used to cover the spectators and keep them cool. There was a strict hierarchy of who sat where; the emperor had his own imperial box, while the front rows were reserved for senators and other VIPs. Behind them sat wealthier Romans, then soldiers, then the common citizens. The very top rows were for people from the lowest level of society – women and slaves – if there were enough spare seats.

Externally Assessed Units

The games at an amphitheatre were paid for either by the emperor or by an ambitious magistrate who, wishing to run for higher political office, hoped to gain popularity by putting on a spectacular show. It was an excellent opportunity for him to be seen by the people and to show that he shared their interests.

Wild beasts

The programme for the day's events at the Colosseum would usually start with displays of wild beasts. There were various ways in which these animals might be used:

- Some animals were trained to **perform tricks**, just as circus animals do today. Roman writers talk about teams of panthers drawing chariots, elephants kneeling before the royal box and tigers licking the hand of their trainer who had just been whipping them.
- Different types of animals were set to **fight one another.** So a pack of dogs might be pitted against a lion, a bear against a buffalo, or an elephant against a rhinoceros.
- There were **staged hunts** of animals. Greenery was placed in the arena and men were sent in to hunt, armed with spears, torches, bows, lances and daggers; they were often also accompanied by a pack of hounds.
- Finally there was a one-on-one fight between an animal and a trained fighter called a **bestiarius**. He would be armed with a hunting spear and would have to fight against an animal such as a lion or a bear.

The more obscure the animal in these shows the better – giraffes, elephants, and hippopotamuses were very popular. Tigers and lions were regularly killed; there is even a story of the emperor Commodus personally decapitating one hundred ostriches in one session. The slaughter of such animals made a strong political statement. The rulers of the Roman Empire were showing both that the empire had control over the fiercest beasts of the natural world and that it had power in the far-flung parts of the world where the animals lived, such as Asia, Europe or Africa. Their hunting of these animals was so ruthless that they caused the extinction of some species in certain areas, such as elephants in North Africa.

Executions

The animals also served another purpose. During the lunch hour convicted criminals were brought into the arena for execution. This too was done to create a spectacle. The criminals would be dragged into the arena and animals would be released into the arena. Sometimes the convicts would be tied to a stake and smeared with blood to encourage the animals. On other occasions, they would be left to run free in the arena, so prolonging their death and lengthening the spectacle for the crowds watching just a few metres away.

Gladiators

Originally, gladiatorial fights seem to have been held at the funeral of an aristocratic man; his slaves would have been expected to fight it out to the death in his honour. However, by the time of the Roman emperors, gladiatorial fights could be held for any reason, including celebrating a public holiday or a Roman military victory.

A great deal of hard work went into training the gladiators in gladiator schools (**ludi gladiatorii**). They were normally slaves, prisoners-of-war or condemned criminals chosen for their toughness and physique. Sometimes poor citizens might choose to become gladiators in a desperate attempt to earn money. It took years to train a good gladiator and it was a brutal process. Upon beginning their training, they had to swear the following oath: 'we solemnly swear to obey our trainer in everything. To endure burning, imprisonment, flogging and even death by the sword.' However, during their training, gladiators fought with wooden swords so that there were no fatal injuries. There were different types of gladiator; four of the most common are described below:

- The **samnite** was armed with a crested helmet with a visor, a breastplate, a greave (shin-pad) on the left leg, a large shield and a short sword.
- Apart from the helmet, the **myrmillo** and the **secutor** wore the same armour. The upper part of their body was bare, below which they wore a loincloth and belt. They had a greave on the left leg and an arm guard on the right arm; they carried a curved rectangular shield like

Externally Assessed Units

that of a Roman soldier and a slashing sword. The **secutor's** helmet was plain, while that of the **myrmillo** was crested and was decorated with a fish.
- The **retiarius** was the most distinct type of gladiator. His weapons were based on those of a fisherman, and so he carried a trident, a net and a dagger. His head was bare, while below he wore a belt, loincloth and a shoulder-piece on the left shoulder.

All the different gladiators might fight each other, but the most popular contest was between the lightly armed **retiarius** and one of the heavier gladiators. The **retiarius** relied on his skill and quickness of movement, hoping to be able to catch the opponent in his net (where he would spear him with his trident). The other gladiators relied on brute force to kill the **retiarius**.

Each show started with a grand parade of gladiators, who were dressed in gold and purple and walked around the arena accompanied by trumpeters. They halted at the emperor's box and said: 'Hail Caesar! We who are about to die salute you.' Once the fighting commenced, the crowd roared for their favourite. Trainers stood nearby, accompanied by slaves holding whips. If the trainers felt that the gladiators were not fighting hard enough, then they would whip them until they improved their efforts.

A fight continued until one of the two was seriously wounded. At this point, trumpets were sounded and a trainer restrained the winner. His defeated opponent could now appeal for mercy to the emperor, who would listen to the opinions of the crowd and then indicate to the victorious gladiator with his thumb. However, that is all that we know. It is uncertain whether 'thumbs up' meant 'let him live' and 'thumbs down' 'let him die', or vice versa. Another theory suggests that he made the sign of a cutting sword with his thumb if he wanted the loser to be killed. Ultimately, we will never know exactly what happened. The significant point, however, is that at this moment the emperor was showing his people that he had power over life and death, and so they should fear and respect him.

If a man had fought well, he would probably be spared; if not, the victor was allowed to cut his throat. The dead body was then dragged out of the arena by an official dressed as Charon, the god who guided the dead into the Underworld. In practice, however, it was not common for a gladiator to be killed – when a gladiator died, it was a waste of all the time and money which had been spent on training him.

If a gladiator had had a distinguished career and fought well, he could earn his freedom and retire from fighting. He would be given a wooden sword to symbolise this. Some gladiators, however, returned to the arena either because they needed the money or missed the excitement. Indeed, some gladiators became immensely popular – women especially admired them and saw them as sex symbols, even buying little bottles of their sweat as keepsakes.

1. Why do you think crowds enjoyed watching other human beings suffer so much?
2. In what ways were the games at the amphitheatre of political benefit to the emperor?

Chariot racing

The greatest stadium in ancient Rome was the Circus Maximus, whose capacity has been estimated at 250,000 people, about five times that of the Colosseum and more than twice that of the largest sports stadium in the world

The Circus Maximus.

today. Chariot racing was actually the most popular sport in the city (rather than gladiatorial shows) – it was followed with the same tribal fervour with which football supporters follow their teams today.

As in the amphitheatre, the circus games were paid for by the emperor or a magistrate hoping to gain popularity with the people. However, the seating plan in the Circus Maximus was far less structured than in the Colosseum. There was a royal box and seats for important citizens, but apart from that people were free to sit where they chose, and men, women and children could sit together. The track itself was about 600 x 200m and covered in sand; it was divided by a long central barrier (**spina**), at each end of which there were three turning posts (**metae**) made of gilded bronze.

The day's events began with a starting procession, where trumpeters and flute-players played while the chariots drove around the arena. Behind them marched soldiers carrying images of the gods – and in particular of Neptune, the patron god of horses. To prepare for the first race, each chariot took its place in one of the twelve starting cages (**carceres**). The race began when the presiding magistrate dropped a white handkerchief; normally there were seven laps of the track in an anti-clockwise direction. The number of laps completed was indicated to the spectators by seven large wooden eggs – each time a lap was finished an egg was lowered (later seven model dolphins were used as well). Races lasted for about 15 minutes and there could be 24 races in a day. Chariots were normally drawn by four horses, although two, three, six and seven horse teams sometimes took part.

There were four teams – the Reds, the Whites, the Blues and the Greens, each of which had its own stables, trainers and fanatical supporters, who wore the colours of their teams and bet heavily on the results of races. Both the charioteers and the horses could become very popular – the emperor Caligula liked one horse in the Green team so much that he gave it a marble stall, purple blankets and jewels. He even claimed that he wanted to make it consul! At the end of a day's racing, there was a prize-giving, where each winning charioteer was awarded a victory palm, a crown, and a golden neck chain.

Most charioteers were slaves; they could become very popular and win enough money to buy their freedom. One such man was Diocles, originally a slave from

Spain, who raced for 24 years and earned so much money that he became the Roman equivalent of a multi-millionaire. However, charioteers could die very young – racing was a dangerous sport, particularly because deliberate fouling was allowed. If a chariot crashed a man might be caught up in the reins and be dragged to death or run over by following chariots. Most accidents happened turning around the **metae**.

It is not hard to see the appeal of the races for the Romans – they were able to support their own team, bet on the results (betting was actually illegal but no one took any notice of this), have a day off work and meet up with friends. The noise of the crowd during a race must have been enormous. The love poet Ovid even tells us of another reason why the games were so popular – as men and women could sit together, he thought it was a great opportunity for men to chat up women they found attractive!

What would you have most enjoyed about a day at the chariot races?

1.3 Homer, The Odyssey

Your *Odyssey* reading includes some of the best stories. Book 5 is where Odysseus is held prisoner by Calypso. In Books 6 and 7 he is washed up in the land of Scherie, where, thanks to Nausicaa, the princess, he is looked after and given safe passage home by King Alcinous. In Books 9, 10 and 12, before leaving, he relates his adventures to Alcinous and tells of monsters such as the Cyclopes, the Laestrygonians, Scylla and Charybdis, and of Circe, the witch.

The *Odyssey* as an epic poem

An epic poem is a long story about a hero who has many adventures as he sets out to achieve his goal. Odysseus' goal is to get back home to Ithaca after ten years of fighting at Troy.

A Greek vase representing someone giving a recitation.

The *Odyssey* was composed to be listened to. Imagine a grand hall after dinner. With a lyre to accompany him, someone is reciting in a chanting sort of voice a long poem about the adventures of a hero. The poem is so long that it would take about 24 hours to hear the whole of it in one go, so the diners listen for a few hours each evening.

For the audience, the poem has to have one clear storyline, in this case Odysseus' journey home to Ithaca. It also has to have memorable characters and description which brings the scenes alive, whether it is an everyday domestic activity or an encounter with a fantastic monster. It must have some serious ideas to ponder over, and some excitement. Will the hero stay and marry the young girl who has found him by the river? Will he escape from the cave of the giant? Will he get turned into a pig?

1.3 Homer, The Odyssey

The poet has to ensure that the characters are easily recognisable and that there are clear stages in the plot, which will allow for rests during the story-telling. It is essential that he keeps his audience alert by making them feel suspense, fear, or pity; and that the poem doesn't become monotonous. Certain words and phrases are repeated, and set scenes recur – such as the sun rising or welcoming a guest – as though the poet has worked out a formula which fits the rhythm of the verse and can be reused in different situations.

The Homeric hero

Before we study Odysseus in detail, let us look at what characteristics a hero had in Homeric times. The hero:

- is physically impressive, and is often described as god-like
- is fiercely loyal to his home and kingdom and longs to be home
- is expected to get retribution if he or his family has been wronged
- commands respect and loyalty from those around him
- is wealthy (wealth is important to a hero because it is an indication of his standing; wealth won in war is particularly valued as it reflects the hero's performance in battle)
- can endure suffering over a long period
- is supported by gods (the gods support only winners, and so receiving help from a god is a sign of heroism, not of weakness).

> **TAKING IT FURTHER**
>
> Draw up your own list of how you think a hero should behave.
> Your list will be determined by books, films and magazines, and perhaps by obituaries or news stories of heroic actions.
> As you read about Odysseus, measure him up according to your criteria.

Odysseus

Homer uses **epithets**, descriptive words or phrases, when mentioning Odysseus. He is ...

Externally Assessed Units

> long-enduring ▪ lion-hearted ▪ valiant ▪ nimble-witted ▪ much-enduring ▪ patient ▪ ingenious ▪ resourceful ▪ shrewd ▪ great-hearted ▪ favourite of Zeus ▪ noble ▪ long-suffering ▪ good ▪ sacker of cities ▪ heaven-born ▪ son of Laertes ▪ illustrious ▪ man of many tales

🎧 Book 5
Track 1

When we first meet Odysseus he is 'sitting disconsolate on the shore ... tormenting himself with tears and sighs and heartache, and looking across the barren sea with streaming eyes' – probably not your idea of heroic activity! But he is expressing great longing to be home, and such depth of feeling is the mark of a hero. Homer does not give passages of psychological analysis, as a modern author might do. He shows the audience how the characters are feeling by describing their actions.

Then Calypso and Odysseus retire 'to a recess in the cavern and there in each other's arms they found pleasure in making love'. Where is his loyalty to his wife, Penelope, you may ask! He is displaying loyalty to his household by striving to return to Ithaca, and the fact that he is staying with Calypso, a foreign woman, does not compromise that loyalty so far as Homer is concerned.

After Calypso agrees to let Odysseus go, she bathes him and dresses him in sweet smelling clothes. You may not think that being bathed is heroic, but it is an honour for him, and now Odysseus is dressed like a real hero.

He lives up to the epithets Homer gives him in his dealings with Calypso. He is 'nimble-witted'. When she suggests a raft, he retorts: 'I shall not entrust myself to a raft unless I can count on your goodwill', and insists upon her swearing she is plotting no mischief. He is 'valiant'. At the prospect of sailing across the seas he claims: 'I have a heart that is inured to suffering'.

His physical strength and practical ability are obvious in the way he single-handedly constructs himself a boat with all the skill of an experienced shipwright.

During the storm he clings on to a rock, and Athene comes to his aid *because* he is a hero. A lesser mortal would not have been worth attending to. Gods don't help losers!

1.3 Homer, The Odyssey

Book 6
Track 2

In this book we see two extremes. At the beginning, Odysseus is a gruesome figure, crawling naked from the bushes like a wild animal. Thanks to his quick wits, he realises that Nausicaa will be offended if he grabs her knees – the usual way to beg for help. Instead he flatters her, likening her to a goddess and saying what a fine bride she will make one day. His strategy is successful. She helps him, and a little later he is clean and dressed, with his hair hanging thick and curly 'like a hyacinth in bloom'.

Book 7
Track 3

In Book 7 it is not so much Odysseus' actions that show him to be a hero, as the way that others behave towards him. Athene envelops him in a magic mist for his journey to the palace, and Alcinous thinks he might be one of the immortals. He is received kindly, but even so, cunningly avoids saying who he is immediately.

Book 9
Tracks 4, 5

He proudly introduces himself – 'I am Odysseus, Laertes' son. The whole world talks of my stratagems, and my fame has spread to the heavens' – and goes on to tell his tale. We see some contradictions in his behaviour: he is a good leader who divides the plunder from the Cicones fairly among his men, and yet seems unable to get them to leave: 'my fools of men refused'. In the Cyclops' cave the situation is reversed: the men sensibly want to leave after taking the cheeses, but he rashly wants to stay.

In his dealings with the Cyclops, he shows his true intelligence and cunning. He says that his ships are destroyed, so the Cyclops will not think of looking for them. He stops himself killing the giant because he knows that he would not be able to unblock the entrance and escape afterwards; and he plans and executes the blinding of the Cyclops, cunningly using the wine brought as a gift to send him to sleep. He cleverly says that his name is Nobody, thus making sure that, if asked, the Cyclops will say that Nobody is hurting him!

He is cunning and brave in organising the men's escape. Realising that the Cyclops would check the backs of the sheep, he lashes his men underneath.

Externally Assessed Units

He himself escapes last, dangerously clinging to the underside of a ram. Unfortunately, however, after all these heroic acts, he lets his anger get the better of him. Against the advice of his men he boastfully announces his name to the Cyclops, thus enabling him to call down curses from his father, Poseidon.

Book 10

Track 6

Odysseus' heroic manning of the sails for nine days and nights means that just as they near Ithaca he falls asleep from exhaustion, giving the crew the opportunity to open the bag of winds. We must ask ourselves why they distrust him so much. In the land of the Laestrygonians he leaves his ship outside the harbour, which means that he can make a quick getaway whilst his men are being massacred. Should we think of him as a coward for deserting them, or as intelligent for escaping while he can?

On Circe's island we see his heroic qualities. He is favoured by the gods and so is provided with a huge stag with which to feed his men, and a drug to make him immune from Circe's evil. She, a goddess, finds him attractive and is pleased to take him as her lover.

Book 12

Tracks 7, 8

We are made aware of Odysseus' heroic status as Circe wonders at his ability to go to the Underworld and return alive. She warns him of the dangers to come, but in recounting her warnings to his men, he wisely leaves out the more frightening details. He hears the song of the Sirens and escapes, thanks to Circe's advice rather than his own ingenuity, and gives his men a good rousing speech as they row past Charybdis. He has been told not to attempt to fight Scylla, but cannot resist putting on his armour ready for a fight. This is a heroic action, but one which puts his men at risk. He is lucky to escape with just six casualties.

After the horror of Scylla, they come to the Island of the Sun, and he lands there, persuaded by Eurylochus' complaints that the men are tired. He is being kind to his men, but it is a foolish decision, because he knows that their 'deadliest peril' lurks there. After the men have been duly punished for killing the cattle, he finds himself back at the whirlpool of Charybdis. We have a splendid example of his quick wits and physical daring as he escapes being dragged under by swinging up into a fig tree and clinging on all day like a bat, until the remains of his ship are thrown up from the depths in the evening.

1. 'In Book 9, Odysseus shows himself to be a real hero.' Do you agree with this statement?
2. 'Obstinate fool', Circe calls him. Do you agree with her assessment of Odysseus?
3. Do you think that Odysseus is a good leader?

> **TAKING IT FURTHER**
>
> Read Book 1 lines 1–90 of the *Odyssey* to find out what the gods think of Odysseus.

The gods

Zeus

He is the ultimate authority: 'When Zeus makes up his mind, it is impossible for any other god to thwart him'. Athene persuades Zeus to instruct Calypso to release Odysseus, and he commands: 'On the journey he shall have neither gods nor men to help him. He shall set out on a raft put together by his own hands, and on the twentieth day, after great hardship, reach Scherie.'

Once Zeus has made a pronouncement, we know what will happen, and wait for the events to unfurl. He is 'the champion of suppliants and guests', but is also the god who punishes those who have acted wrongly. When laws have been broken, he delivers his punishment. The crew stay too long plundering the Cicones, and Odysseus says that the trained fighters who arrive have been sent 'by Zeus to make the men suffer'. He is swift also to punish the men who have eaten the forbidden cattle of the sun: 'Zeus thundered and struck the vessel with lightning … there was no homecoming for them: the god saw to that'.

Athene

Athene is a supporter of Odysseus, and argues for his release from Calypso. Although very powerful, she is aware of the views of the other Olympians, and

Externally Assessed Units

does not always come to his aid: 'Pallas Athene heard his prayer but still refrained from appearing before him, out of deference to her father's brother, Poseidon'.

In Books 6 and 7, Athene is the one who ensures that Odysseus is found by Nausicaa and reaches the palace. See how each of her actions has the aim of helping Odysseus get safely to Alcinous. She:

- tells Nausicaa to do the washing, including men's clothes
- tells her to ride to the river
- makes the maid miss the ball
- puts courage into Nausicaa's heart
- makes Odysseus taller, sturdier, more radiant
- envelops Odysseus in a thick mist
- appears to Odysseus as a young girl to help him find his way.

Poseidon

The blinded Cyclops, Polyphemus, has prayed to his father Poseidon to bring disaster on Odysseus. 'I mean to let him have a bellyful of trouble yet,' proclaims Poseidon when he sees that Odysseus is on the seas again. Poseidon is a very important god for Homer, because, being the god of the sea, he has the power to cause storms. He can therefore make Odysseus take refuge on strange islands and come face to face with monsters.

Hermes

Hermes appears once in his role as messenger from Zeus, when he tells Calypso that Odysseus should leave her island. Homer makes him seem quite human as he complains about his journey: 'Who would choose to race across that vast expanse of salt water? It seemed unending. And not a city on the way, not a mortal soul to offer a choice sacrifice to a god.'

Odysseus is left to cope with the Cicones, Laestrygonians and Cyclops without divine help, but Hermes appears with advice and the herb moly to help him rescue his men from Circe.

> **Do you think that the gods and goddesses make the *Odyssey* more or less exciting?**

1.3 Homer, The Odyssey

Women

In a world where women are generally quiet and subservient to men, the women in the *Odyssey* are a spirited and intelligent bunch. Calypso keeps Odysseus prisoner and Circe changes his men into pigs. Nausicaa is only a young girl, but has the confidence to give him instructions, and her mother is bold in questioning him about his clothes.

The reactions of the women to Odysseus are a measure of the hero's greatness. Calypso loves him and offers him marriage and immortality, Circe immediately wants to take him to bed and then turns into a kindly mentor, and Nausicaa drops a few hints about how he would make a handsome husband.

We must note, however, that many of the monsters that threaten Odysseus are female: the Sirens, Amphitrite, Scylla and Charybdis.

Calypso

Calypso's name comes from a Greek word meaning conceal, and she conceals Odysseus for seven years. This may be Homer's way of keeping Odysseus away from Ithaca, thus giving Telemachus time to grow up before his father's homecoming. She is the daughter of Atlas and therefore divine. She is the 'Nymph of the plaited hair' and 'Nymph of the lovely locks'.

When we first meet her, she is carrying out the traditional woman's occupation of weaving, and singing as she works. She kindly offers Hermes hospitality, but straightaway asks him why he has come, and is bitter when he gives her the message from Zeus that Odysseus must leave.

She feels it is unfair that she is going to lose: 'a man whom I rescued from death … I tended him … I offered to make him immortal and ageless'. She will obey Zeus, she says, but 'I will not help him on his way'. However, she promises: 'with a good grace and unreservedly to give him such directions as will bring him safe and sound to his native land'.

She approaches the weeping Odysseus with the news that he may leave – 'my unhappy friend, don't go on grieving' – giving the impression that it is her goodness of heart that has prompted her to release him. He is suspicious of her offer to help him, fearing that she is plotting mischief. She responds with

Externally Assessed Units

affection to the 'crafty' way his mind works. She, however, is no less crafty, and has a final attempt at keeping him with the promise of immortality.

She keeps her word as she helps him to prepare for his departure, by providing him with the materials and tools with which to build a boat. She does not help him though. Perhaps she hopes that the task will be too much for him and he will have to stay! When the boat is built and he is ready to set out, she is the perfect hostess: she bathes him, provides him with clothes and gives him wine, food and – thanks to her divine powers – a gentle breeze to blow him in the right direction.

Circe

Circe is well-known as the witch who changed Odysseus' men into pigs with her magic potion, and then kept Odysseus on her island for a whole year. Like Calypso, she is divine, but appears quite human in her singing, weaving, and domestic arrangements.

However, do her noble deeds far outweigh her witchery? Once she has recognised that Odysseus is able to resist her powers, and has sworn to him that she will do him no harm, she becomes a model hostess. Her maids set out a meal and prepare a bath, and Circe herself washes Odysseus, rubs him with olive oil and gives him splendid clothes. After a whole year of feasting, when Odysseus says that he wants to leave, she does not hinder him. She shows her divine wisdom by telling him that he has to visit the underworld, giving him precise instructions.

On his return she is the 'glorious goddess' who greets him with bread, meat and wine. She foretells his next encounters – with the Sirens, and Scylla and Charybdis – and gives him instructions on how to survive them. She warns him to avoid at all costs harming the Sun-god's cattle. Like Calypso, she gives him a favourable wind.

Homer calls her the 'formidable goddess'.

Nausicaa

In a dream, Athene gives Nausicaa the idea of taking a wagon down to the river to wash clothes, suggesting to her that she may soon be married and need clothes for herself and her groom. Not only does Athene thus ensure that Odysseus will get clothes, but also that Nausicaa will be interested in him as a potential husband.

1.3 Homer, The Odyssey

The 'tall and beautiful princess' is, however, much more than an agent of Athene. In her, Homer creates a charming and realistic character. With her father she acts like any cunning daughter asking a favour – 'She went close to her dear father and said: Father dear, I wonder...' She is too shy to mention her own new-found interest in clothes for marriage, but gets out of him the wagon she wants. As she eats the picnic her mother has prepared, or throws off her headgear, plays ball and sings, she is a typical carefree young girl having fun. However, we see her as very practical and capable as she takes the whip and flicks the mules or sets about doing the washing.

This intelligent, sensitive and capable young woman is well up to the challenge of dealing with a naked man emerging from the bushes! At the sight of him she is the only one to stand firm. She is sharp enough to understand that with his likening her to the goddess of chastity, and his pitiful tale of sufferings at sea, he is not about to attack her. We can believe too that his references to her as a bride will not have gone unnoticed! As a civilised princess she knows that 'all strangers and beggars are under the protection of Zeus', and immediately extends hospitality in the form of food, drink, a bath and clothes.

She is practical in making arrangements for Odysseus' journey into the city, asking him to make his own way there as she does not want to attract gossip. The fact that she relates to him in detail the things people might say – 'Who is this tall and handsome stranger with Nausicaa? Her future husband, no doubt!' – is a broad enough hint to him about what is in her mind!

But of course she will not marry him, and at the end of the day she returns to her own apartments, where a fire is lit for her and supper prepared in an inner room by her nurse, her mission accomplished and adventure over.

Does this painting by Frederick Leighton (1879) match *your* idea of Nausicaa?

Externally Assessed Units

Arete

Arete is a caring mother who packs a picnic for her daughter's trip to the river, but also a powerful woman. Nausicaa says of her: 'If she is sympathetic to you, you may confidently expect to see your friends again'. And we are told: 'She is also a wise woman, and when her sympathies are enlisted she settles even men's disputes'. Odysseus is given firm instructions that he should walk straight through the hall: 'Till you reach my mother who sits in the firelight by the hearth, spinning yarn dyed with sea-purple – a marvellous sight'.

After such a build-up, it is perhaps rather surprising that Arete seems to play little active part in the acceptance of Odysseus, though she does recognise the clothes he is wearing and questions him about them.

1. 'Women are the source of many of the difficulties for Odysseus in the *Odyssey*.' How far do you agree with this statement?
2. 'It is mostly thanks to help and good advice given by women that Odysseus overcomes the obstacles on his journey.' Do you agree?

Other characters

Alcinous

We are told that Alcinous is divinely inspired, that he is 'Mighty Alcinous' and that he sits drinking his wine like a god. His sons look like immortals. With his generous hospitality towards the stranger Odysseus, he represents true civilised behaviour.

He is also a loving father who understands his daughter's embarrassment at talking about marriage, and is happy to give in to her request for a washing trip to the river.

In Book 8 he arranges for Odysseus to be carried home to Ithaca, despite the prophecy that some day Poseidon would wreck one of their vessels (which he does in Book 13).

Polyphemus and the Cyclopes

Before we meet the Cyclopes we are told that they are fierce and lawless: they don't cultivate the land or build boats, have no laws and are not sociable.

1.3 Homer, The Odyssey

They have nothing in common with the values represented by the civilised Odysseus. Before Odysseus meets Polyphemus, the signs are that he is dealing with an unfriendly giant: his cave is in an isolated position and has a high entrance. The interior of the cave is, however, surprising, as this giant seems to be extremely well organised. He has baskets laden with cheeses and all his lambs and kids are penned up separately. His vessels are well-made and swimming with whey, and he milks his ewes methodically. This good housekeeping is not what we expect of a monster!

When we finally meet him, he enters with a dramatic crash, throwing down his firewood, and then gets down to his tasks. He discovers the intruders and Odysseus treats him as though he is a civilised person, reminding him of the laws of hospitality sacred to Zeus. Polyphemus makes it clear that he cares nothing for the gods, and then questions Odysseus about where his ship is moored. We see here that, though an uncivilised monster, he is cunning. Odysseus responds with equal cunning, saying that his ship is lost, but Odysseus' clever words are no defence against Polyphemus' next act – the barbaric devouring of two of his men.

The next morning we see again the two sides to the Cyclops' character: one minute he is efficiently milking his ewes, the next breakfasting on two more men.

That evening Odysseus uses the wine he had brought as a gift, to make Polyphemus drunk and incapable, and so the Cyclops' rejection of **xenia**, the laws of hospitality, will prove to be his downfall. He makes the cruel joke to Odysseus that his gift is that he will eat Nobody last, and then passes out. Homer surely wants us to feel no pity for him as he describes the revolting scene: 'a stream of wine mixed with morsels of men's flesh poured from his throat'.

Red-figured storage jar representing Odysseus blinding Polyphemus.

Externally Assessed Units

There are, however, moments when we might feel some sympathy for him, for example when the roots of his eyeball crackle and he gives out a dreadful shriek. He seems a pathetic character when, 'tortured and in terrible agony', he addresses his favourite sheep: 'Sweet ram ... you must be grieved for your master's eye', whilst the cunning Odysseus hangs on underneath its belly.

However, in the end it is the blinded Cyclops who has the last word. Odysseus, in boastfully calling out his own name, gives Polyphemus the information he needs, and he calls upon his father Poseidon to curse 'the sacker of cities'. The boulder he throws misses the ship, but the anger of Poseidon will prove more deadly to Odysseus and his men.

The Sirens

Sea journeys are full of danger, and many cultures have stories of figures (usually female) who lure sailors to their deaths. Circe warns Odysseus that the Sirens sit in a meadow piled high with skeletons and bewitch everyone who approaches them. It is her idea that he should strap himself to the mast and block his crew's ears with wax if he wants to hear their song and live. Homer vividly describes him as 'gesturing with his eyebrows' as, bound to the mast, he begs his deaf crew to release him.

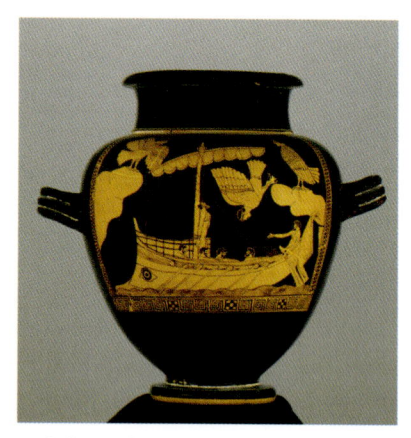

Red-figured storage jar representing Odysseus and the Sirens.

Scylla and Charybdis

Scylla, with her 12 feet dangling in the air, lives in a cave overlooking the straits which Odysseus must pass through. She preys on passing sailors. This she can do easily because she has six long necks and heads with a triple row of fangs with which to snatch them. Homer makes her particularly sinister by describing her strange bark. It is a dreadful sound, but no louder than the yelp of a new-born puppy. She strikes silently before Odysseus sees her.

When Scylla strikes, Homer concentrates not on the monster, but on the scene from Odysseus' perspective. He sees only arms and legs dangling high in the

1.3 Homer, The Odyssey

air above, and feels helpless as the men call out his name for the last time. The emphasis on dangling limbs, together with the sounds of the men calling and shrieking, makes this scene particularly vivid.

Charybdis is the whirlpool on the other side of the straits. The human terms that Homer uses to describe it (or *her*, rather – it is a female monster) express its horror very strikingly. She sucks, vomits, swallows and roars.

Homeric values

Xenia or 'guest friendship' is the bond of solidarity between guest and host, an essential code of conduct in the ancient world. You never knew, as a traveller, when you might have to throw yourself on a stranger's mercy if you were stranded. The host was bound to provide accommodation and gifts, and the guest to respect the host and offer gifts in return. The guest is invited to tell his story, but only when he has finished eating.

We can see examples of **xenia** throughout the *Odyssey*. It is honoured by all the civilised characters we meet:

- By **the gods:** Calypso instructs Hermes: 'First follow me inside and let me offer you hospitality ...' When he has dined and refreshed himself, he answers Calypso's questions.
- By **Nausicaa** when she meets the destitute Odysseus: 'But come, girls, give the stranger something to eat and drink.'
- By **Circe**, although at first her motives are far from honourable! 'I followed her indoors and she offered me a beautiful silver-studded chair with a stool for my feet. She prepared a brew in a golden bowl for me to drink.' She then happily entertains Odysseus and his men for a year.

Giving the guest a bath, as Calypso does for Odysseus, is also part of **xenia.**

Odysseus in vain reminds the Cyclops of his obligations: 'Good sir, remember your duty to the gods; we are your suppliants, and Zeus is the champion of suppliants and guests. He is the god of guests: guests are sacred to him.'

In elder points out to Alcinous when Odysseus arrives at the palace: 'It is unseemly and unlike your royal ways to let a stranger sit in the ashes at the hearth ... tell him to get up and sit on one of the silver chairs, and tell your

Externally Assessed Units

squires to mix some more wine ... and let the housekeeper give him a meal from all she has available.'

Xenia extends to giving the traveller what he needs to continue his journey, and so Alcinous pronounces: 'We will safeguard him on the way from any further hardship.' Aeolus gives Odysseus the bag of winds.

Civilisation and barbarism

Following the rules of **xenia** is the mark of a civilised people. The Phaeacians are an excellent example, as we see in Nausicaa's response to the arrival of Odysseus: 'This man is an unfortunate wanderer who has strayed here, and we must look after him, since all strangers and beggars come under the protection of Zeus.'

In the Cyclops' cave we see a reversal of **xenia**, as Odysseus' men are not fed, but eaten. We are prepared for this behaviour by Homer's introduction to the Cyclopes: 'a fierce lawless people who never lift a hand to plant or plough' and 'who have no assemblies for making laws, nor any established legal codes'.

The barbarity of the Laestrygonians is graphically illustrated by the picture of the men carried off for dinner 'like fishes on a spear'.

Some acts carried out by Odysseus may seem uncivilised to us today, but were acceptable in the Homeric heroic code. Odysseus needs to feed his men, and is therefore justified in taking what he needs from the Cicones.

Homer's narrative and descriptive technique

Direct speech makes the stories dramatic and brings the characters to life. Much of the *Odyssey* is made up of speeches. For example, in Book 5 we have the dialogue between Calypso and Odysseus when she tells him he may leave. In Book 6 there is Odysseus' clever speech to Nausicaa and her thoughtful response to him, and her instructions to her maids. All of Books 9, 10 and 12 are in Odysseus' words, and within his story he uses direct speech.

Epithets are descriptive phrases which stress a person's characteristics and help to establish them in the memory. Nausicaa is the 'white-armed', a quality of well-born women. Odysseus is 'sacker of cities' and 'illustrious' – reminders that he is a hero and to be admired.

1.3 Homer, The Odyssey

Recurrent phrases or formulae no doubt originally helped the oral poets to compose and remember their material. Phrases such as 'as soon as dawn appeared, fresh and rosy-fingered' and 'the whole day long till sundown we sat down to a feast of unlimited meat and mellow wine' are found throughout the story.

Small detail helps readers to imagine the scene and become more involved in the story. Sometimes, the detail creates a sumptuous scene: 'Golden statues of youths, fixed on solid pedestals, held flaming torches in their hands to light the banqueters in the hall by night …' At other times the detail expresses the horror of the scene, for example the 'unwatered milk' with which the Cyclops washed down his meal of human flesh, or the sound as the Cyclops' eye 'hissed round the olive stake in the same way that an axe or adze hisses when a smith plunges it into cold water'.

Similes are used at moments of great drama. They are often taken from nature, and present a vivid picture in themselves. Odysseus' boat is driven 'like the north wind at harvest-time tossing about the fields a ball of thistles that have stuck together'. His men are carried off 'like fishes on a spear' or float 'like sea-gulls on the waves'. Odysseus emerges from the bushes 'like a mountain lion who sallies out, defying wind and rain in the pride of his power, with fire in his eyes to hunt down the oxen or sheep or pursue the wild deer'.

Gruesome detail shocks the audience, and their sense of horror makes them listen more intently. Polyphemus 'seized a couple and dashed their heads against the floor as though they had been puppies. Their brains ran out on the ground and soaked the earth'. We shudder when, 'seizing the olive pole, they drove its sharpened end into the Cyclops' eye'.

Scene-setting gives a clear picture of the location of an event, rather like a stage set. The description of Calypso's cave is an example of a vivid setting: 'trailing round the mouth of the cavern was a thriving garden vine, with great bunches of grapes; from four separate but neighbouring springs four crystal rivulets were channelled to run this way and that'.

Irony is used to increase the suspense. Alcinous fears that one day Poseidon's prophecy will come true, and one of his vessels will be wrecked; the audience suspects that it will be the vessel that has carried Odysseus. The audience is

65

Externally Assessed Units

aware that Odysseus, in triumphantly shouting his name to the Cyclops, is giving him the very information he needs in order to harm him.

Pathos means making the audience feel sorry for the suffering of the characters, and so getting them more involved in the story. For example, Scylla's victims 'shrieking and stretching out their hands ... in their last desperate throes'. In Telepylus, the 'groans of dying men could be heard above the splintering of timbers'. We don't easily forget these desperate cries.

1.4 Ovid, Metamorphoses

The *Metamorphoses* contains over 250 transformations. You are studying three (1, 3 and 8) of the 15 books which make up the poem. Book 1 starts, logically, with the biggest metamorphosis of all, the creation of the world, and goes on to tell stories about the gods. In Book 3 the stories are related to the city of Thebes, and it is King Minos of Crete who is the link which binds together the stories in Book 8.

Ovid as storyteller

Fantastic transformations feature widely in children's stories and legends today. Ovid, 2000 years ago, would also have grown up knowing folk tales about magical shape-changing, and, to produce the *Metamorphoses*, he added to them stories he had come across in Greek and Roman poets.

Writing a poem you can't read to anyone is exactly like making gestures in the dark.

Ovid wrote these words when he was living on the Black Sea, far away from Rome. He had been banished there by the Emperor Augustus, and although he could still write poetry, he was stuck in a barbarian country where nobody could understand or appreciate his work. These lines are a reminder that his poetry was written primarily to be listened to, and not read silently.

Storytelling was a much more popular occupation for ancient Romans than it is for us, since we have so many different forms of entertainment. Imagine Ovid's poetry being recited after dinner to amuse guests.

You will notice how important nature is in the poem – rivers, springs, the wind, the sea, trees and hills. People in Ovid's time lived much closer to nature than we do, and probably would have experienced the fear of being caught in a storm at sea, the pleasure of finding a cool stream in the hot countryside, or the magical stillness of a hidden grove.

The idea of metamorphosis

The word **metamorphosis** means a change of form, and this shape-shifting is the thing which unites all the different stories in the poem.

Externally Assessed Units

Why do people change shape?

Ovid describes many different situations. The metamorphosis can be:

- An explanation for the existence of an object, for example the pan pipes, the eyes in the peacock's feathers or the evergreen laurel.
- A release from an unpleasant situation, where the victim appears happy to accept the change. Daphne prays for an escape from Apollo, and happily waves her branches and nods her head in the treetop.
- A just punishment. Scylla deserves to be a small bird torn at by a falcon, and Erysichthon is justly treated for callously felling the sacred tree.
- A cruel punishment from a god. Actaeon, Pentheus and Semele suffer undeserved, cruel deaths.
- A gift from a god as a reward for piety. Philemon and Baucis are granted their request and stay together as trees growing side by side.
- At the will of the shape-changer and a reversible process. For most, the change is final, but Mestra can change when she wants.
- A reflection of the personality of the person who has been changed. The violent Lycaon is transformed into a wolf.
- A pretend metamorphosis. Daedalus and Icarus imitate birds in order to escape from King Minos in Crete.

The speed and detail of the metamorphosis

Some transformations happen 'off stage', and come as a surprise to the audience. Nisus, for example, suddenly appears in bird-form to attack his daughter – 'her father had lately been changed to a falcon'. Ovid gives us no other information about this change. He tells us in detail about Narcissus' sufferings, but the flower springs up without warning.

On the other hand, the reader witnesses some transformations in great detail:

Daphne's Track 10 'soft white bosom was ringed in a layer of bark, her hair was turned into foliage, her arms into branches'. As she is changing into a tree Apollo offers her evergreen leaves, and the glory of being entwined in his hair. 'With a wave of her new-formed branches the laurel agreed, and seemed to be nodding her head in the treetop'. Daphne has been granted her wish to remain a virgin, and Apollo retains contact with her in a metamorphosis that brings them both some sort of satisfaction.

1.4 Ovid, Metamorphoses

The detailed description of **Actaeon**'s metamorphosis allows us to experience the horror he feels: 'She (Diana) changed his hands into hooves and his arms into long and slender forelegs'. He has lost all control as he 'bolted, surprising himself with his speed as he bounded away'. What makes this metamorphosis so cruel is that he maintains his human awareness but cannot communicate. The final act of callousness on the part of the goddess is to make his own dogs attack him, whilst his companions ironically encourage them and regret that Actaeon himself is not present to witness such a 'heaven-sent prize'.

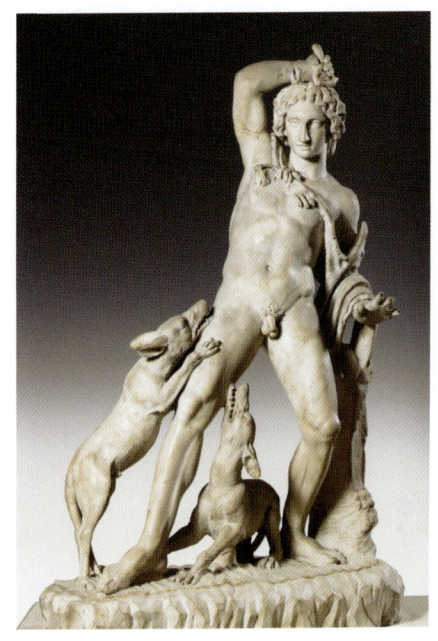

Actaeon is torn apart by his own dogs in this sculpture.

Baucis and Philemon Track 20 witness each other 'sprouting leaves on their worn old limbs', but for the old couple it is not alarming, for it is what they had asked for from Jupiter. And so as they change at a moderate speed it is not their shock or anxiety that we see, but an old couple ready for death who fondly say goodbye to each other before, in perfect synchronisation, they change into an oak and a linden and remain together for eternity.

Some metamorphoses are humorous, for example, the wicked and scornful **Lydian sailors** being transformed into dolphins. One mocks another before realising that he too is changing: 'whilst he was speaking, his own mouth widened, his nose protruded and all of his skin grew hard and scaly'. We smile to see these arrogant pirates getting the punishment they deserve.

1. How does Ovid stop the repeated act of metamorphosis becoming boring?
2. 'For some characters, metamorphosis is a happy release'. Choose two stories and show how they illustrate this statement.

The characters

The *Metamorphoses* is crammed full of all sorts of characters: gods, minor deities and mortals; monsters; males and females; old and young; good and evil. Some are portrayed in detail, others we have only the briefest encounter with. Some characters are there to provide a useful link between stories. One way of approaching the characters is to divide them up according to how happy or sad, guilty or innocent they are. We find:

- Admirable characters who have a happy ending
- Innocent victims of the gods
- Victims manipulated by a god
- Sons cursed from birth
- Victims of their own emotions
- Immoral characters who deserve to be punished
- Characters who provide a useful link between stories.

Admirable characters who have a happy ending

These characters are the moral examples we should, perhaps, follow. They do their duty towards the gods and get rewarded for their piety.

Deucalion and Pyrrha. Track 9 'You'd never find a better or more right-minded man than Deucalion, neither a more god-fearing woman than Pyrrha, both of them guiltless of sin and both devout in their worship'. Their piety means that they are chosen by Jupiter to be the sole survivors of the flood and the ones to re-people the earth. They are devoted to each other: 'If you were lying beneath the waves, my beloved, I should follow you there to be drowned beside you'. Their honest, matter-of-fact reaction to being the only people in the world, 'an inglorious crowd of two', is touching yet slightly ridiculous. Ovid gently pokes fun at them as Pyrrha trembles, and they both prostrate themselves before the Oracle. When the Oracle gives an answer, poor Pyrrha is totally bewildered at what seems to be a command to commit an impious act, but then mightily impressed by her husband's interpretation of it. Finally we see our little old couple stepping out, scattering the stones that will metamorphose into people.

Philemon and Baucis. Their story is introduced as proof that the gods' power is boundless, since Jupiter destroys their impious neighbours, but gives them

1.4 Ovid, Metamorphoses

eternal companionship as a reward for their piety. Ovid gently pokes fun at them too. We imagine the great gods having to stoop to enter their humble house. We witness Baucis rushing around trying to make the house look respectable, and bringing out the best things, her hands shaking in her anxiety to get things right. The drapes are worn, the table is wobbly and has to be levelled, and the crockery is rough earthenware, but she still does her best. Ovid describes the succession of dishes of simple foods as though they are a banquet, and all is going well until the old couple notice that the wine-mixing bowl keeps refilling itself. They know it must be the work of the gods, and hasten to make a sacrifice, not knowing that the king of the gods himself is in their house. The only animal they have to sacrifice is the goose which guards their home. The bird refuses to be caught, and we get a farcical picture of the old couple getting exhausted as they chase it; finally the gods admit who they are and the bird is saved.

The gods tell them: 'walk in our footsteps up to the mountains'. There is humour in the picture of them wearily climbing 'the long steep slope' using their walking sticks. The gods can walk rather more speedily than the old couple! Philemon and Baucis seem to take everything in their stride. They witness their home being changed into a temple, and their one request is to die both at the same time. Ovid tells us that they are standing 'casually' in front of the temple one day telling the sanctuary's history, when they both start to sprout leaves. There is no fuss; they say farewell to each other and the metamorphosis is completed, turning them into an oak and a linden which will grow side by side for ever.

Innocent victims of the gods

Io _{Track 11} runs away from Jupiter, but he 'stealthily raped her' and then, to avoid detection by Juno, changes her into a heifer. To make things worse, Juno, suspicious, sends Argus to guard her. It is Io's terrible inability to communicate that Ovid stresses. 'When Io wanted to supplicate Argus with outstretched arms, no arms were there to outstretch. When she opened her mouth to complain, her own voice startled her; all that emerged was a hideous lowing.'

Her new form frightens her and makes it impossible for those who love her to recognise her: 'When she saw her reflected head with its strange new horns, she recoiled from herself in a panic'. She came to the banks where often she had played. The naiads had no idea who she was, and even Inachus failed to

Externally Assessed Units

know her'. She pathetically follows those she knows, and Inachus, 'plucked some grass and tenderly held it out to her. Licking and kissing her father's hands, she couldn't help weeping'. When finally she writes her name with her hoof, we witness his suffering at her inability to respond. 'All you can offer me back is a melancholy low,' he laments.

Even when her metamorphosis is eventually reversed, Ovid stresses her innocence and timidity: 'frightened to speak, in case she still lowed like a heifer, she nervously tried a few words in her long-lost language'. If Ovid is laughing at her, he is doing it with understanding and affection.

Daphne is another innocent girl who has a tender relationship with her father and suffers from the unwanted attention of a god. Both Apollo and Daphne are victims of Cupid's arrows: he has been made to fall in love, she to repel love. Ovid describes Daphne as running joyfully through the woodland, free and happy until Apollo catches sight of her. He pursues her, on fire with love, she flees as swift as a breeze. There is humour in his ridiculous promise that if she doesn't run too fast he'll slow down too. Apollo tries to reassure her that he is not a wolf pursuing a lamb, but the more he tries to explain, the faster she runs. And the faster she runs the more attractive her exposed limbs and flowing hair are to him. Soon Ovid is likening him to a hound snapping its jaws at a hare. 'His breath was ruffling the hair on her neck. Her strength exhausted, the girl grew pale'. It seems that there is no escape for Daphne, and she prays desperately to her father to help her escape.

Apollo pursuing Daphne, as represented by Gianlorenzo Bernini.

The effects of her prayer are immediate, and she starts to turn into a tree. Our first response is to feel sorry just for the girl, whose hair is now foliage and arms branches, but Apollo is a victim too. He is a pathetic figure: 'caressing the trunk

1.4 Ovid, Metamorphoses

with his hand, he could feel the heart still fluttering under the new bark'. The last we see of Daphne is her branches nodding in agreement as Apollo tells her that her evergreen leaves are 'for glory and praise everlasting'. Her metamorphosis is not altogether unwelcome.

Victims manipulated by a god

Teiresias, **Semele** and **Echo** cause their suffering through their own actions, but cannot really be held responsible since a god has outwitted them. **Teiresias'** original crime, the thing which caused his first metamorphosis, was the killing of two snakes, for which he was turned into a woman. In Book 3 he is a man again. He has been blinded by Juno as a punishment for betraying women's secret, but has been given the gift of prophecy by Jupiter as compensation. It is the fact that he is a prophet that interests Ovid, because it allows the poet to introduce other stories by making the link with his powers as a seer.

Semele _{Track 13} is already pregnant by Jupiter when we first meet her, and is about to become the victim of Juno's plotting. She is naïve – 'Semele's unsuspecting mind was already persuaded by Juno's suggestion' – and this leads her to ask Jupiter to appear to her in all his glory. 'Her mortal frame was unable to take the celestial onslaught' and so she is consumed by Jupiter's firebolt.

Echo has already been cursed by Juno for helping Jupiter with his various affairs, and has fallen in love with Narcissus. For the audience the interchange between Echo and Narcissus is comical in its misunderstandings. But there is no humour as the nymph flees with the pain of rejection, or in the picture of her wasting away in the cave until all that remains is voice and bones.

Sons cursed from birth

Narcissus _{Track 14} will be safe as long as he 'never knows himself'. He is attractive but arrogant. His rejection of all his admirers builds up to the climax of his falling in love – with himself. We feel pity for his hurt, and frustration that his love is hopeless, but if he had not been so absorbed in himself he might have fallen in love with somebody else (such as Echo!).

Meleäger _{Track 18} is blinded by his love for Atalanta, and this leads him to present her with the boar as a trophy, thus denying his fellow hunters their reward.

Externally Assessed Units

Echo and Narcissus, a painting by John William Waterhouse.

When faced with their anger, 'grinding his teeth in rising fury' he plunges his sword first through one uncle's heart, and then the other's. At this point in the story he is presented by Ovid as little more than a rather thoughtless young man, blinded by his sudden infatuation for Atalanta whose favour he wants to gain. Our sympathy is roused for him, however, as: 'he bravely mastered the terrible pain', his death all the worse for being brought about by his own mother's actions.

Even before he sets out on his journey to find his sister, **Cadmus** Track 12 is bound to have trouble, for Juno's hatred for Europa has been transferred to her kinsfolk. He is pious, consulting the Oracle at Delphi, and making offerings when he finds the heifer. We see how brave he is as he dons a lion skin and tackles the dragon. Ovid uses Cadmus' family and the city of Thebes, which he founded, as a link between the stories in Book 3.

Pentheus Track 15 has rudely rejected Teiresias' wise warnings, and when Bacchus arrives in Thebes he refers to his worship as 'this juggler's tricks' and his followers as 'effeminate eunuchs'. Bacchus punishes him in the cruellest of ways. His mother, in a frenzy induced by the god, and thinking he is a wild boar, attacks him with her sisters. He admits his 'impious wrongdoing', but too late. His aunts tear off his limbs, and it is a pathetic picture Ovid gives of Pentheus: 'He had no

1.4 Ovid, Metamorphoses

more arms to extend to his mother. All he could show was the wounded stumps of his sundered limbs as he yelled out "Look at me, Mother!".' He has undergone a metamorphosis, but only in the eyes of those attacking him. The panic he shows is not unlike that of Actaeon who is attacked by his own dogs. The gods show no mercy to humans who lack respect!

Victims of their own emotions

We feel sorry for **Daedalus** _{Track 17}, when he witnesses his son Icarus plunge from the sky. The next story, however, tells of a previous action of Daedalus. He had murdered his nephew Perdix because he was jealous of his inventions. There is perhaps a message here, or at least a sort of poetic justice. Perdix is changed into a bird which is afraid to fly. It was his love of flying that made Icarus go too near the sun and plunge to his death.

As Ovid describes **Althaea** _{Track 19}, the repeated opposites reflect the dramatic conflict which is tormenting her. Her speech as she debates whether she should kill her son is full of anguish. Two names pull at her single heart: her cheeks are pale, her eyes red; her expression is cruel and then compassionate; her tears are dried up and then gush again; her anger is quenched and then rekindled. Finally she tosses the log on the fire, bringing death to Meleager, and then kills herself.

Scylla _{Track 16} is an engaging study in how obsession turns a young girl who has been innocently playing on the walls into a scheming murderess, a kind of metamorphosis in itself. When war breaks out, she watches the fighting and catches sight of Minos. Before long, 'beside herself with excitement', she has fallen in love with him. He, of course, has no idea that he is being observed, let alone that a whole scenario that will end in death is evolving in Scylla's mind. Ovid amuses us by tracing her train of thought in detail. He must have been thinking of the arguments he had heard in rhetoric classes or in the law-courts as he makes her justify her actions.

The first Minos knows about Scylla's plans is when she appears before him in the night, clutching her father's lock and declaring her love. When he recoils at her behaviour and rejects her, she becomes angry, shouting in fury and calling him a traitor. Finally, he leaves and as she clings to his ship, she is attacked by her father, now metamorphosed into a falcon. She herself then changes into a bird.

Externally Assessed Units

The interest in this story is not so much the metamorphosis as the content of Scylla's speech. Romans would have been amused by the echoes in it from Dido in the *Aeneid* and Medea in Euripides' tragedy.

Immoral characters who deserve to be punished

Erysichthon Track 21 callously cuts down an old oak tree sacred to Ceres, ignoring the blood pouring from its bark and the groans it utters. He even lops off the head of a servant who objects to what he is doing. We feel that he deserves his punishment of constant, desperate hunger. Ovid pushes his hunger to a ridiculous extreme as he finally starts to 'bite his own limbs'.

However, Ovid does not give us a simple moral tale of crime and punishment. Erysichthon has a daughter whom he sells to get money for more food, and thanks to a gift from Neptune, she is able to metamorphose into 'a bird or a mare or a cow or a deer' and escape from her new owner to be resold for more food. There is an element of black humour in this con trick.

A 21st century metamorphosis? What stories might the Romans have come up with to explain this man's warts?

Characters who provide a useful link between stories

Minos is the innocent victim in the Scylla story. Ovid makes him a central figure in Book 8 through his links with Scylla, Daedalus and Theseus.

Cadmus has his own story as he valiantly fights the dragon, and he also links together the other Theban characters in Book 3.

---

1. What other categories can you put the characters in? You could, for example, divide them up according to which god causes their metamorphosis or whether they are male or female.
2. Narcissus, a mythological character created 2000 years ago, is so well described by Ovid that we could quite easily meet someone like him today. What details does Ovid include to make him so realistic?

1.4 Ovid, Metamorphoses

> **TAKING IT FURTHER**
>
> Draw a chart showing all the characters that undergo a metamorphosis. Use the following headings:
>
> - Character
> - Reason
> - Changed into
> - Deserved?
> - By which deity

Relationships and emotions

Above all, Ovid was interested in passion. Or rather in what a passion feels like to the one possessed by it. (Ted Hughes in his introduction to *Tales from Ovid*)

A brief survey shows us the range of emotions which feature in our stories.

Tender affection is seen in the elderly happy couples Deucalion and Pyrrha, and Philemon and Baucis. Daedalus cares deeply for his little son as he warns him how to fly safely, and the fathers of Io and Daphne show compassion towards their daughters whom they love deeply.

Sadness and pain often follows the cruel behaviour of others. Echo, 'wretched and sleepless with anguish', is one of the saddest characters.

Fear is well conveyed by Ovid as Pentheus and Actaeon try to flee their attackers.

Frustration comes over strongly as Actaeon and Pentheus try to communicate their identity to save their lives, and Echo tries unsuccessfully to speak. Apollo too is powerless as he presses his lips to the wood, but the wood still shrinks from his kisses, and so is Narcissus when he gets no response from the boy in the reflection.

Love is sometimes unrequited, as in Apollo's for Daphne, or Echo's for Narcissus. Sometimes it is the hot passion like that which Scylla has for Minos, Pan for Syrinx, Jupiter for Io or Narcissus for himself!

Jealousy causes Juno to punish Io, Semele and Echo.

Anguish is explored in great detail in the story of Althaea, who is torn between loyalty to her son or her brothers.

Externally Assessed Units

Grief – the sisters of Meleäger provide a graphic description of grief as they mourn for their brother.

Obsession takes hold of both Scylla and Narcissus.

Spiteful resentment are words used of Cupid's feelings when Apollo mocks his weapons, but they could apply equally to many other gods. Diana, Bacchus and Juno are all spiteful.

Pride and arrogance bring about the downfall of humans who are punished by angry gods. Pentheus and Erysichthon are good examples.

Pathos is a Greek term for deep emotion, or suffering. Ovid often uses images, language and situations which arouse sadness, sympathy, or pity in his audience.

The metamorphoses usually happen within the context of a family, and Ovid portrays the relationships with great feeling. You will find:

- Father and son
- Mother and son
- Father and daughter
- Husband and wife
- Grandfather and grandson
- Uncle and nephew
- Brothers and sisters.

> Find examples of these relationships in the stories you have read.

Gods and morality

All mortal creatures must yield to a god. (*Metamorphoses* Book 1)

Where did the Romans' gods come from?

The Romans, and the Greeks before them, knew that there were huge outside forces that could ruin them. Crops could be destroyed, sudden storms could wreck ships. If the sky went dark, thundered and then produced violent flashes capable of killing you, something or someone must be angry with you. The something was imagined to be man-like and it had to be kept happy. Once the power had a human form, it was given human emotions, and so stories developed about it.

1.4 Ovid, Metamorphoses

Poets and artists used their imagination and added to the stories. Ovid drew on ideas from Homer, other poets and Greek tragedy when he was composing the *Metamorphoses*. He also drew on paintings of myths and statues of gods.

Why did Ovid write as he did about the gods?

- Was he poking fun at the gods?
- Did he see them as good raw material for his imagination?
- Did he just want to make a written collection of stories he had heard?

The gods

Jupiter or Jove makes his appearance in Book 1 when, having launched his thunderbolt and laid low the giants, he calls an assembly. His power is firmly established: 'he is mightily angry as only Jove can be angry', and all the gods respond at once to his summons. Ovid gives us a picture of him enthroned on a dais clutching his ivory sceptre. The mere shaking of his head causes the earth, sea and constellations to tremble: 'A word and a gesture sufficed to control the murmuring hubbub and all were silent'.

He is a figure of justice when he turns the evil Lycaon into a wolf, a metamorphosis which suits the man's vicious character, and he is just when he grants the pious old couple, Philemon and Baucis, a reward for their piety.

However, he is more often presented in the *Metamorphoses* as a cheating husband who will use any tricks he can to seduce any females he likes the look of. He first entices Io into the woods and rapes her, and then turns her into a heifer in an attempt to avoid detection. He has seduced Europa in the form of a bull, made Semele pregnant, and made love to many a nymph in a mountain dell, with Echo as his look-out.

Juno, his wife, is constantly trying to get her own back on him. She knows him too well, and when it suddenly goes dark in the middle of the day, her first instinct is to suspect Jupiter: 'Where was her husband? She was quite familiar with Jupiter's amorous tricks as she had caught him straying so often'. She pursues his lovers with venom, and seems to enjoy getting her revenge. She 'quietly gloats' over the blow to Agenor's house when Actaeon is killed, since he is a relative of Europa, who is one of her husband's amorous conquests. When she discovers that Semele is pregnant, she has further 'cause for resentment', and takes pleasure in orchestrating her death, 'I must target the woman herself and destroy her'. She is often 'blazing with anger', and we see her 'venting her fury' when Argus has been killed, by 'sending a horrible demon to frighten the eyes of Io by day, and her mind at night'. Teiresias too is a victim of her anger. She resents his answer to a question and in 'disproportionate fury' strikes him blind. She curses Echo because she has helped Jupiter to deceive her.

Other gods too are vindictive. **Bacchus** sends Pentheus to a ghastly death, torn apart by his mother because he doubts the god's divinity. **Diana,** upset that Actaeon has, by accident, seen her naked, changes him into a stag and is pleased to see him attacked and killed by his own hounds. Only when he has been destroyed in 'a welter of wounds' is she said to have cooled her anger. She vents her anger on another occasion too when, not receiving the worship she feels is her due, she dispatches a wild boar through the fields of Aetolia with the cry 'This slight shall not go unpunished'. **Cupid,** angered by a remark by Apollo, in 'spiteful resentment', shoots two arrows, one which makes Apollo fall in love, and another which ensures that Daphne will never return his love. **Ceres** is severe in her punishment of Erysichthon, who has heartlessly and evilly cut own her sacred tree.

Gods sometimes show a sympathetic side. **Neptune** had raped Mestra in the past, but he takes pity on her by helping her to escape her new master. **Apollo** is consulted as the god of prophecy, but his main appearance is as the victim of Cupid's arrow, and in many respects he is as helpless as the human victims. His love is rejected, and he is pitiable as he clings hopelessly to the tree which was Daphne. Jupiter feels sorry for Io.

Ovid is not intent on directly preaching a moral lesson to his readers, but the message comes over clearly that pride will be punished. There is no guarantee, however, that a blameless person will remain safe. Actaeon is innocent but suffers a horrible death: 'why punish a man for a pure mistake?' asks Ovid. He quotes the ancient saying: 'Count no man happy until he is dead and his body is laid to rest in the grave', a reminder that the gods are unpredictable and cruel, and that no human is ever really safe from them.

1. Is the moral of the *Metamorphoses* simply that bad behaviour is always punished?
2. Do you agree that there is little to admire in the behaviour of any of the gods or goddesses?

> **TAKING IT FURTHER**
>
> Investigate some other representations of mythological scenes. You could look at Greek vases, sculpture or Pompeian wall-paintings. Research what happened at traditional Roman country festivals.

Ovid's narrative technique

Spin me a thread from the world's beginning down to my own lifetime, in one continuous poem. (*Metamorphoses* Book 1)

The image of a spider weaving a web is very appropriate: one of the outstanding features of the *Metamorphoses* is the clever way Ovid makes his narrative slip from one story to another. Here are some of the ways he makes the links. Read through one of the books you are studying and spot what type of link he is using.

- A character explains to others why he is about to do something.
- A character is asked by the previous one to tell his story.
- A character moves to a different country, which prompts new stories.
- An article, for example a leaf, prompts a story.
- The next story happens in the same place.
- A relative of the previous character prompts the next story.
- The story illustrates something previously mentioned.
- The previous character's fame is the link.
- A story is told to disprove the previous one.
- A request is made for more stories.
- It is dinner time (where story-telling is traditional).

The *Metamorphoses* consists of a series of short narrative poems, skilfully woven together to form a continuous work, such as the tale of Pan and Syrinx, which

Externally Assessed Units

Mercury tells Argus, or the story of Erysichthon, which is told to convince the audience that the gods do indeed have power and should not be mocked.

Landscape painting

Ovid often sets the scene clearly, with a detailed description of the landscape, rather as a theatre director might design a stage set. This allows him to establish the mood and setting before we meet the characters:

> Picture a valley basin, where streams of rainwater trickle down from the hills to a marshy dell, well-filled at the bottom with pliant osiers, light sedge grass and dense swamp-rushes, withies and tall bulrushes with short reeds growing below.

Small human detail

Sometimes it is the broad landscape picture that entrances us; sometimes, the finest detail:

- Scylla went up to the wall to throw the 'smallest of pebbles'.
- Icarus would 'carelessly soften the yellow wax with his thumb'.
- Atlanta's robe was 'clasped at the neck by a buckle of polished metal, her hair very simply gathered up in a single knot'.
- Baucis and Philemon's drapes were 'brought out only on special occasions'.
- The table leg that was too short and had to be 'levelled with a potsherd'.

These details make us engage with the characters and what they are doing. As we focus on the minutiae of their acts or appearance, so we become more involved with them and the narrative.

The grotesque

In some stories it is the macabre and grotesque which make the narrative so gripping. The dragon which Cadmus encounters is fearsome:

> The veins swelled full on his bloated throat, his jaws with their poisonous fangs were dribbling with yellow white foam, his scales rasped as they scraped the soil, and his hellish mouth, panting with foul black breath, infected the air with pollution.

This small part of the description of the dragon alone shows how well Ovid appeals to the senses of the reader – we see the terrible jaws, and can also hear the panting and smell the foul breath.

1.4 Ovid, Metamorphoses

Rhetoric

Learning how to talk persuasively was a part of every well-born Roman boy's education. Ovid, as a young man, had decided that poetry was for him, not the serious world of the law-courts. However, in the *Metamorphoses* we can recognise several speeches which use the techniques Ovid must have practised in school, and these speeches are an important part of his narrative technique. Most of the story of Scylla is expressed through her long speeches. The first one is to herself as she tries to persuade herself that going down to offer herself to Minos is the correct course of action. The other is when Minos has rejected her and she wants to prove his guilt by showing that she is the innocent party.

Direct speech

The use of direct speech helps to make the stories come alive. As Cadmus is sowing the dragon's teeth, the armed men don't just appear, but one of them surprisingly tells him off: 'Leave those arms! This is a family feud. You stand aside!'

As Daphne is being chased by Apollo, it is the direct speech which makes the story so dramatic. Apollo, whilst chasing her, manages to deliver a long speech in which he begs her to be careful. 'How frightened I am that you'll fall and scratch those innocent legs in the brambles. You mustn't be hurt on account of me.' And he suggests to her 'Don't run so fast and I promise to slow down too.' The irony of the words is not lost on the reader, for it is Apollo himself who is frightening her and causing her to run with such desperation! Daphne's plea to her father, by contrast, comes over as genuine and heartfelt: 'Help me father. If rivers have power over nature, mar the beauty which made me admired too well.'

It is the desperate words 'Autonoë, help me! Actaeon's ghost is pleading for mercy!' which bring Pentheus' tragic situation to life and emphasise the horror of his death.

Personified abstractions

Ovid takes an abstract power and gives it the form of a human. The most striking example, perhaps, is Hunger in Book 8:

> Her hair was tangled, her eyes like hollows, complexion pallid, her lips grimy and grey, her throat scabrous and scurfy. Her skin was so hard and fleshless, the entrails were visible through it; her shrunken bones protruded under her sagging loins.

Externally Assessed Units

Notus, the South wind, is described in a similar way in Book 1: 'with his beard a bundle of rain-storms'.

In this way Ovid makes us aware of the tremendous power of these abstract forces.

Similes

Ovid sometimes uses similes to bring his narrative to life. Some are about nature and belong to the tradition of epic poetry; others relate specifically to Roman things which his contemporaries would have known well. Some add humour or pathos to the description.

'The men-turned-dolphins frolicking gaily like dancers, wantonly tossing their bodies, spreading their nostrils to shoot the seawater fountaining upwards.' Likening the villainous sailors to dancers conveys well the movement of the dolphins/men, but also adds a hint of scorn, for these hard and ruthless sailors would hardly want to be seen as frolicking dancers.

'His fist brought up a crimson weal on his naked torso, like apples tinted both white and red, or a multi-coloured cluster of grapes just ripening into a blushing purple.' This is how Narcissus' breast is described when he has beaten it in desperation. The simile expresses the colours, but to choose ripening fruit also gives the idea of both beauty and vulnerability. Narcissus is heading for unavoidable tragedy, just as ripening fruit must eventually decay.

Some similes have a much more Roman flavour and are taken from things familiar to Ovid's contemporaries (and which would not have been around in the mythical times in which the stories are set). We are told of the boar: 'Fire flashed forth from his eyes and the breath of his nostrils was flame. As a massive rock that is forcefully flung from the sling of a catapult flies through the air to demolish a wall or a tower full of soldiers.' This reference would have been particularly vivid for the Romans who had served in the army.

The theatre, too, was a common experience for civilised Romans. Ovid uses a theatrical image to get his audience to imagine the men strangely sprouting from the dragon's teeth. 'Think of a tapestry front cloth rolling up in the theatre at festival time. The embroidered figures slowly and smoothly ascend, their faces first and then the rest of their bodies.'

Humour

In the midst of all these tales of death and tragedy, Ovid still makes us smile. The excessive grief of Meleäger's sisters is presented humorously: reckless of all decorum, they bruise their breasts with their fist-blows, and as they cling to the gravestone they sprout feathers and all but two of them are turned into guinea-fowl.

When Daphne has been chased by Apollo and then changed into a laurel tree, the bewildered rivers don't know whether they should congratulate, or offer condolences to, her father.

Erysichthon is evil and deserves his punishment, but there is something amusing about the way he keeps selling his daughter, who promptly undergoes a metamorphosis and escapes her new master each time!

Philemon and Baucis are characters who display great piety, and are to be respected for their kindness towards Jupiter and Mercury, but they do appear rather farcical as 'they set out to placate their mysterious guests by killing the goose, their only one, which guarded the tiny farm; but the bird kept fluttering around, exhausting the elderly couple and long eluding their grasp ...'

The gods, too, despite their cruel ways, are portrayed with humour. When Juno notices that it has suddenly gone dark in the middle of the day, she immediately suspects Jupiter: 'Where was her husband? She looked all around. She was quite familiar with Jupiter's amorous tricks, as she'd caught him straying so often.' The humour continues as she outwits him by asking for the heifer (Io in disguise) as a present. 'What was he to do? To surrender his love would be cruelly painful, but not to give her would look suspicious.' The reader is pleased to see that his trick has backfired on him and enjoys his dilemma.

The description of the boar hunt is farcical. Nestor pole vaults and ends up in a tree, Telamon gets his foot caught and falls on his face, Ancaeus, wielding his two-headed axe, boasts 'leave this to me', and is promptly gored by the boar, and Jason hits a poor innocent dog by mistake!

Externally Assessed Units

Tragedy

There are reminders of Greek tragedy in the moments of great drama, as in Book 8 when Queen Althaea realises that her son has killed her brothers. She wants to avenge them, but that means killing her own son. She knows that if she destroys a certain log her son will die: 'she ordered her servants to lay some pinewood and kindling, and then she applied the fatal taper. Four times she withdrew it. A conflict raged between mother and sister'. Ovid gives her an emotional speech in which she debates what she should do and shows her great distress at having to make such a decision: 'I wish for his death, but am powerless, confused! One moment I picture my brothers' wounds and that scene of murderous carnage; but then my spirit is broken by love and the name that I own as a mother.'

Epic

Ovid and his readers were familiar with Homer's *Odyssey* and *Iliad* and Virgil's *Aeneid*. These were epic poems which told of wars and heroic actions, and at times the *Metamorphoses* sounds like a grand epic poem.

The bloodthirsty and grotesque description of the wounds inflicted by and on the Calydonian boar reads like a battle scene from the *Iliad* or *Aeneid*. 'Ancaeus collapsed; his bowels burst out in a seething mixture of gore and gut, and the earth beneath him was soaked with his blood.' Another feature of epic is the long catalogue of names, such as the 33 hounds that attack Actaeon. The poem in Latin is written with the same verse form as epic (hexameters) and this would enhance the epic atmosphere for the ancient audience.

1. How does Ovid keep the reader absorbed in the story he is telling?
2. How well does the story of Cadmus and the dragon illustrate Ovid's technique as a story teller?

1.4 Ovid, Metamorphoses

> **TAKING IT FURTHER**
>
> Ovid was born in the year after Julius Caesar died and wrote the *Metamorphoses* when Rome was flourishing under the Emperor Augustus. When we read the *Metamorphoses* we are aware of the greatness of Rome. The poem begins with the creation of the world (the big metamorphosis of the earth as we know it from chaos) and ends with the metamorphosis of Julius Caesar into a god: just as Jupiter governs the heavens, 'so earth is under Augustus; and each is father and ruler'.
>
> The assembly of gods in *Metamorphoses* Book 1 is described as though it was a meeting of important Roman politicians on the Palatine Hill, where the Emperor Augustus had his house. The minor gods are on the edges of the meeting, like the plebs, the less important citizens of Rome. The more important gods are closer to the chief god, Jupiter. Ovid seems to want his readers to imagine that Augustus is as great as Jupiter.

1.5 Sparta

Sparta was a unique society. It had developed differently to any other Greek city-state and by the 5th century (the high point of Greek civilisation) it was a military state which caused fear and suspicion among other Greek peoples. During this century, it established a fierce rivalry with Athens, the other super-power of the Greek world, which culminated in the famous **Peloponnesian War** between the two cities (each supported by their respective allies). When Sparta won this conflict, it was briefly the most powerful city in the whole Greek world, even though its dominance lasted only for 33 years until it was defeated by the Thebans.

Spartan society was so brutal that we still use the adjective 'Spartan' to mean 'tough' or 'harsh'. One modern historian has even described Spartan warriors as the 'Samurai' of the ancient world. So how did this remarkable society develop?

The geography of Sparta

One factor in the development of Spartan society was its geographical location. The city of Sparta and its surrounding region, **Laconia**, was situated in the south-east of the Peloponnese peninsular in southern Greece (see map). The city itself was located in a deep valley through which flowed the Eurotas river. The valley was bounded by mountains on both sides. The geography of the region provided two key advantages for its inhabitants:

- **Food resources**. The valley was very fertile, and particularly suitable for fruit and olive-growing, while the Eurotas river provided a plentiful supply of fish. In addition, the forests of the adjacent mountains were teeming with wild animals – Spartans were famous for their love of hunting.
- **Defence**. The geography of the Eurotas valley created a natural defence system for the city. The mountains could be crossed only through a series of narrow passes, while to the south the coastline of Laconia was rugged and marsh-ridden. As a result, it was very difficult for Sparta's enemies to attack either by land or sea, while the Spartans could keep a tight control on who entered and exited their territory.

1.5 Sparta

Map of the Peloponnese.

The origins of Spartan society

The emergence of a city in Sparta can be dated to between the 11th and 9th centuries BC. During these years, the Greek world underwent dramatic changes; new Greek speaking peoples from the north of Greece invaded and settled the lands to the south, often expelling the original inhabitants. These new invaders were known as **Dorian** Greeks, while the original inhabitants were known as **Achaean** Greeks.

When Dorian invaders arrived in Laconia, they soon settled in the area around Sparta. By the beginning of the 8th century, they had taken control of the whole of Laconia. The Spartans then had to decide how to treat the other inhabitants of Laconia. They allowed other Dorian inhabitants a degree of self-government; they called these people **perioikoi**, or 'those who live around'. However, they treated the remaining Achaean Greeks far more harshly. They were captured, enslaved and forced to work as serfs on Spartan farms; these serfs were known by the Spartans as **helots**, or 'captives'.

It didn't take long for the Spartans to expand their regional control. They soon invaded the fertile region of Messenia to the west of Laconia (see map).

The vast majority of the conquered Messenian population were enslaved as helots and forced to work for their Spartan masters; as a result, Spartans were now outnumbered by helots by a ratio of at least 10:1. However, the Messenians did not submit easily. In the middle of the 6th century they rebelled and fought the Spartans for most of the next 20 years. It was a brutal war, and the Spartans won only with enormous military courage and sacrifice.

This war, called the Second Messenian War, came to define Spartan society in the centuries which followed. Sparta realised that, since it would always be vastly outnumbered by its helots, it could hope to be successful only with sustained and brutal suppression of these slaves. It was at this point that Spartan society seems to have changed dramatically.

Tyrtaios

Sparta's national poet, Tyrtaios, was writing during the Second Messenian War. He wrote war poetry which encouraged soldiers to fight bravely and sacrifice their lives for the city. The following lines are typical:

> Let us fight with spirit for this land and let us die for our children, no longer sparing our lives ... Make the spirit in your heart strong and valiant, and do not be in love with life when you are a fighting man.

As Spartan history progressed, Tyrtaios' poetry came to express the military ideals of the city. Spartan warriors sang Tyrtaios' poems and songs around campfires for generations after his death.

The evidence

One of the main problems faced when studying Sparta is the lack of first-hand evidence of their society. This is partly because the Spartans discouraged their citizens from writing things down. Therefore, where Athens has left us with the works of historians, playwrights, poets and philosophers, there is hardly any written evidence from the people of Sparta. This means that we can only go on what outsiders have told us about the city; many of them were probably biased against what to them was a foreign and threatening society.

Various Athenian writers of the 5th century give us details about Sparta. The historians **Herodotus** and **Thucydides** tell us about the city's role in the Persian and Peloponnesian wars respectively. Some comedies of **Aristophanes** set during the latter war sometimes make fun of the Spartans, while the historian **Xenophon** tells us much about Spartan society at the beginning of the 4th century. Writing a few years later, the philosopher **Aristotle** informs us about Sparta's political system. However, perhaps the most important source of written material about Sparta was the much later historian and biographer **Plutarch**, who wrote a biography of **Lykourgos** (see below) in the 2nd century AD. Yet by this time early Sparta must have seemed like ancient history to him and so we cannot be sure how accurate his information is.

The Spartans did not believe in constructing glamorous buildings, in contrast to Athens. Thucydides commented that if the city of Sparta were to be deserted and only its foundations remained, then 'future generations would find it very difficult to believe that the place had really been as powerful as it was meant to be'. We have very little archaeological evidence from Sparta, and this makes understanding Spartan society even more challenging.

Lykourgos

After the Second Messenian War, Spartan society underwent a radical social revolution. Spartans liked to believe that this revolution was led by a man called Lykourgos, a noble Spartan who oversaw the changes that the city needed to make in order to keep control over the helots. However, Lykourgos is a puzzling figure for historians, and some even doubt whether he really existed. Nonetheless, the Spartans certainly believed in his existence, and they looked to him as their founding father. So what did they believe that he had done?

The story went that he had travelled to the oracle at Delphi to get instructions from the gods about how to reform Spartan society. The system he came up with became known as the **Spartan System**. These are some of the most important changes which he made:

- **A professional army**. Lykourgos apparently decided that all Spartan citizens should become full-time soldiers and spend their lives training for war, so that they were always able to overcome any threat from the helots. The Spartan army was therefore the first professional army in Greek history.
- **An education system**. To develop the future generations of Spartan warriors, Lykourgos established a state education system which trained boys from the age of 7 to become outstanding soldiers. He also established

Externally Assessed Units

a system of education for girls, so that they too would serve the state as effectively as possible.

- **Equality**. Lykourgos observed that there was great inequality of wealth and land ownership between Spartan citizens, but he believed that they would only fight for each other if they all felt equal. Therefore, he tried to make all Spartan citizens equal in wealth – they were all given a plot of farmland of the same size and an equal number of helots to work it. They were not allowed to build grand houses and they had to eat together every evening in dining-clubs. To symbolise their new equality, Lykourgos gave Spartan citizens a new name: **Homoioi**, which meant 'Equals'.
- **Government**. Lykourgos was given instructions about how to reform the government of Sparta (see page 99).

> How difficult do you think it would have been for Lykourgos to persuade the Spartans to accept his reforms?

Spartan social structure

During the 7th and 6th centuries BC, the concept of **eunomia** (good order) was being developed in Greek city-states. This referred to a well-organised political system, with citizens obeying its laws. Guided by Lykourgos, Sparta came up with its own version of this concept: the three-tiered social structure. At the top were the Spartan citizens, known as **Spartiates** (**Spartiatai**) or **Homoioi** (see pages 99–102 below). Below them were the **perioikoi** and at the bottom of the pile were the **helots**.

The perioikoi

The **perioikoi** probably had a reasonable quality of life compared to many other peoples in the Greek world. As long as they obeyed their Spartan masters, they were allowed to get on with life in their own communities. Their most important role in Sparta was as craftsmen and traders, since **Spartiates** were forbidden from engaging in these activities.

There were probably about 100 communities of **perioikoi** scattered around the less fertile regions of Laconia, and their villages acted as a buffer zone to prevent **helots** from escaping from Sparta.

- **Origins:** Dorian settlers living around Laconia.
- **Political status:** They lived in self-governing communities, where they had local citizenship. However, they were allowed no role or say in Spartan government.
- **Rights/duties:** Their chief contribution to Spartan life was economic – they were traders and craftsmen of materials such as clothing, shoes, furniture, storage pots, metalwork, while communities living near the coast also engaged in fishing and shipbuilding. They were also expected to serve as soldiers alongside **Spartiates** during times of war.

The helots

The **helots** suffered greatly in the Spartan system. Since they outnumbered the **Spartiates** by at least 10:1, they were subjected to brutal repression for centuries. Their main role was to work on the Spartan farms, while **helot** women did the domestic work required in a household.

- **Origins:** Either conquered Messenians or original Achaean inhabitants of Laconia.
- **Political status:** state-owned slaves who had no political rights.
- **Rights/duties:** They had to farm Spartan lands and supply a fixed amount of produce annually to their **Spartiate** masters. They were able to keep or make a profit from any surplus produce. They were also required to act as servants to their **Spartiate** masters in times of war (as skirmishers). **Helot** women acted as household slaves and were famed for being good nurses for babies.

The **helots** were treated extremely harshly. At the beginning of each year, the magistrates of Sparta declared war on them; this meant that it was legal for a **Spartiate** to kill a **helot** at any time. Sources also relate that **Spartiates** used to force **helots** to get drunk in order to warn young Spartans about the dangers of drunkenness. They were also humiliated by being forced to sing ridiculous songs, to dress up in animal skins, and to receive regular public beatings 'so that they would never forget that they were slaves'. They were also the targets of the brutal **Krypteia** (see page 95).

Helots could also be freed for outstanding acts of courage or service on military campaigns, although this could actually be dangerous. The historian Thucydides tells a story of the freeing of **helots** who had fought bravely in a battle against the

Athenians in 424. The Spartans invited the bravest 2,000 **helots** to step forward after the battle and receive their freedom. However, every single one of them disappeared soon afterwards – almost certainly murdered by their Spartan masters, who wanted to eliminate such brave men from their society.

> **Can you think of other societies either today or in the past which have had a similar social structure to Sparta?**

Spartan education

The Spartan education system devised by Lykourgos aimed to make each Spartiate a superb and unquestioningly loyal soldier.

The early years

Babies received tough treatment right from the beginning of their lives. New-born babies were inspected by a committee of elders and, if considered deformed or too weak, they were left to die of exposure on the slopes of Mt Taygetus. If they survived this test, they had to endure a harsh infancy. Babies were not allowed to be wrapped in swaddling clothes, were bathed with wine, not water, as this was thought to be a test for epilepsy, while they were often left in the dark on their own. As they grew, children were not allowed to be fussy about their food.

Aged 7–14

At the age of seven, a Spartan boy was sent off to the city's boarding school known as the **Agoge** ('Rearing'). He would never live with his family again. The boys lived in communal barracks and were divided into packs, each led by prefects, known as **eirenes**. The **eirenes** were 19 or 20 year old Spartans who had recently graduated from the **Agoge**. The Headmaster of the school was known as the **Paidonomos**, and he was always a Spartan warrior with a great record.

The boys were under constant supervision and the **eirenes**, who were armed with whips, could punish the boys for any offence. The boys did not learn much reading or writing – only enough to train them for basic literacy. Nor did they study any literature and philosophy, unlike Athenian boys. Instead, a great deal of time was spent developing physical strength and obedience. Music was also an important aspect of their education. By learning to compete in choral competitions, the boys were taught the value of precise movement and teamwork, which would be vital in battle situations when they were grown up.

Aged 14–18

At this point, the really intensive training started! Youths were trained to go barefoot at all times so that they could run faster, scale heights more easily and clamber down cliffs. They were allowed only one cloak for the whole year, whatever the weather. They had to cut their hair short and generally played naked – their bodies became tough and were unused to baths and lotions; they enjoyed such luxuries only on a few special days a year. Food was deliberately rationed to make them used to doing without it on a military campaign if necessary. As a result the boys were forced to steal to get more. If they were caught, they were beaten 'for stealing carelessly'.

Aged 18–19

It is not exactly clear how young Spartans progressed into the adult world at the age of 18. However, it seems that students now became **eirenes** and some would act as pack leaders for the younger members of the **Agoge**. Despite these new responsibilities, the youths were still kept under constant pressure to behave properly. The historian Xenophon tells us that, when walking in the streets, the youths were forced to stay silent and keep their eyes fixed on the ground ahead of them. It is also likely that at this age some Spartans were enlisted into the **Krypteia** – Sparta's secret police force.

The Krypteia

The **Krypteia** was a well-kept secret by the Spartans, and much of its activity remains a mystery to this day. However, the historian Plutarch (see page 91) does give some information about the organisation. It seems that the strongest graduates from the **Agoge** were selected to serve for a period of time in hiding (**Krypteia** means 'Hiding'). They were sent out into the countryside of Laconia and Messenia, where they were given minimal rations so that they had to live off the land. During the day they lay low, but at night they patrolled the land and – most significantly – they were encouraged to kill any helot they thought presented a danger to Sparta. After a period in the **Krypteia**, young Spartans were trained and efficient killers who knew how to terrorise the helot population.

> 1. How does Spartan education compare to the education you are receiving?
> 2. How do you think Spartan boys felt about their education system?

Spartan citizens and the army

The whole of a **Spartiate**'s adult life was spent in training for war. In fact, Plutarch tells us that their life in training was even tougher than when they were actually at war. They spent their whole time hunting, training and competing in musical competitions. Until the age of 30 (when **Spartiates** tended to marry), they were not allowed to live apart from their companions but slept in army barracks.

- **Origins**: Original Dorian conquerors of Sparta.
- **Political status**: A privileged social class holding all political power.
- **Rights/duties**: They had to have graduated from the **Agoge** and to have been elected to a dining-club (see below). They became full citizens aged 30 and were also known as **Homoioi**, or Equals, to emphasise that they were all equal in Spartan society. They had equal political and legal rights and were given a farm by the state, with helots to work it. They were forbidden to engage in farming, trade and industry.

The syssition

One of the key features of the **Spartiate** lifestyle was the dining-clubs. In order for a young Spartan to gain full citizenship after leaving the **Agoge**, he had to be elected into a dining-club, known as a **syssition**. Each **syssition** had about 15 members and they were expected to eat together every night. When on campaign, they also shared a tent together.

The election process for a new member was as follows: each member was allowed to vote on a new candidate by dropping a ball of bread into an urn.

If any member was opposed to the candidate, he squeezed his ball flat and the candidate was rejected. However, if the candidate was elected, he became a member of the **syssition** for life, and had to provide a fixed quota of rations from his farm each month.

The Spartan army

Since Spartans spent their whole lives training for war, the Spartans developed the most feared army in the Greek world, which was undefeated in war for almost 300 years. The key to their success was their mastery of the **phalanx**, a style of fighting which had emerged in the 7th century – the Second Messenian War is one of the first wars where the **phalanx** tactic is recorded.

A **phalanx** was a rectangular formation of soldiers in rows and columns – each column was usually eight rows deep. In the front row, the soldiers advanced together at the same pace, with their shields raised in their left hands; each soldier therefore relied on the shield of the man to his right to protect his right side. When they met the enemy, each soldier thrust forward his long spear into the lines of opposing soldiers. If a man in the front row fell, then the next man in the column behind him stepped forward to take his place.

Spartan hoplite.

Externally Assessed Units

A successful phalanx required each soldier to know his place and to stand his ground in company with his colleagues. This is where all the Spartan training came into its own. Music was also central to the **phalanx**, as orders were communicated not by shouting but by a piper playing different tunes. This is why musical training was so important to Sparta's military success.

The heavily-armed soldiers of the phalanx were known as **hoplites**, a name which came from their weapons, or **hopla** in Greek. The key offensive weapon was the long spear (about 3 metres in length), but a **hoplite** also carried a short sword, which he would use if he lost his spear or fought at close quarters.

The Battle of Thermopylae

The battle of Thermopylae remains the most famous battle in Spartan history, even though the Spartans were eventually defeated there. In 480, the whole of Greece was being invaded by the huge Persian empire to the east. All the main Greek cities joined together to meet the Persian invasion; they decided that the best place to do this was at the small pass of Thermopylae in central Greece, where the mountains came down to within a few feet of the sea; this therefore made it very easy for a small number of men to hold back a large army. The Persian army was indeed massive – some estimate that it was between 100,000 and 200,000. By contrast, the Greeks had a mixed force of just 7,000 to defend the pass, led by 300 elite Spartan warriors and their King Leonidas.

For two days, the Greek forces managed to slaughter thousands of Persians in the pass. Although the Persians had many more soldiers, they were lightly armed compared to the Greeks and were no match for the Greeks' **phalanx** formation. The Persians were finally able to get through the pass only when a local Greek, Ephialtes, betrayed his countrymen (in return for a vast payment) by telling the Persians about a mountain path which led to the other side of the pass. On the third morning of the battle, the Greeks realised that they would soon be trapped from both sides in a pincer-grip. Leonidas dismissed most of the Greek allies, so that only the 300 Spartans and some other local Greeks remained. They fought bravely to the death that day, holding up the Persians for another few hours.

1.5 Sparta

Although the battle was ultimately a defeat for the Greeks, it had two positive effects on the subsequent war:

- **Buying time:** first, it bought the Greek allies a few extra days to prepare for the Persian invasion of the south of Greece. This they did by abandoning Athens and moving as many Greeks as possible into the Peloponnese peninsular.
- **Morale:** secondly, the battle gave the Greeks a tremendous morale boost by showing them that such a small number could stand up to and kill vast numbers of Persians. This was a crucial factor when the Persians next arrived in the south of Greece – the Greek navy had the self-belief to pull off a stunning victory in a sea-battle off the island of Salamis.

Leonidas.

The best way to learn to learn about the battle of Thermopylae is to read the account written by the Greek historian Herodotus in his *Histories* (VII.207–239). One of the key figures in events was the Spartan ex-king Demaratus. In the build up to the battle, the Persian king Xerxes was advised by Demaratus, who had been deposed and forced to flee from his homeland; as a result, he decided to defect to the Persians. Herodotus' account of Demaratus' advice tells us a lot about what the Spartans believed about their army. You can read what he says in Herodotus' *Histories*, VII.101–105, 209, 234–235.

1. List the reasons why you think the Spartan army was so successful.
2. Why do you think that the syssition was so important to Spartan society?

Spartan government

The Spartan system of government consisted of four different bodies which each had different roles in the constitution. The four were the two **kings**, the five **ephors**, the **Gerousia** (a council of 28 elders), and the **Ecclesia** (the assembly of Spartan citizens). The system of government was designed so that no single body had too much power and each was closely supervised.

The kings: the two kings were equal constitutionally, preventing one of them from becoming too powerful. There were two royal families, the **Agiads** and the **Eurypontids**, each of which provided one king. It was believed that both families were descended from the Greek hero Heracles. The kings' powers and duties were as follows:

- **Military leaders**. The most important role of a king was to lead an army in the field and act as commander-in-chief. Only one king would be sent on a military campaign.
- **Religious leaders**. They were believed to be the priests of Zeus and led important religious ceremonies.
- **Limited judicial powers**. They had a limited role in the Spartan legal system, being responsible only for cases involving the adoption of children, the marriages of orphaned heiresses and the control of public highways.

The kings were given some privileges. For example, their children didn't have to go through the **Agoge**, they were served their meals first at their **syssition**, and the whole state observed ten days' mourning upon their deaths. On the other hand, they were also closely scrutinised. The **ephors** were responsible for supervising them and ensuring that they governed according to the laws. Two **ephors** also accompanied the king on a military campaign and reported back on his leadership. In addition, if the people had any complaints about a king's performance, he could be deposed (as Demaratus was).

The ephors: five new **ephors** were elected each year by the **Ecclesia**. Any **Spartiate** could stand for election, but an **ephor** could only serve once in his lifetime, which meant that none of them gained any long-term power. Their most important responsibilities were as follows:

1. presiding over the **Ecclesia**;
2. supervising the performance of the kings;
3. acting as judges in some law cases;
4. dealing with foreign ambassadors;
5. declaring war on the **helots** at the beginning of each year and choosing the members of the **Krypteia**;
6. running the education system and choosing the **Paidonomos**.

1.5 Sparta

The Gerousia: a body of 30 men: the two kings and 28 **Spartiates** over the age of 60, who served for life. They acted as advisers to the kings, but their most important role was to prepare bills to be presented to the **Ecclesia** for them to vote on. They could propose bills on foreign policy, changes in the law and matters of war and peace. However, if they didn't agree with the way in which the **Ecclesia** had voted, they were able to reject its decision. They also acted as a court and jury to try criminal cases and could administer punishments, which included the death penalty, banishment or the levying of fines.

A new member of the **Gerousia** was elected in a rather strange ceremony. When a vacancy came up for one of the 28 places, candidates were brought into the **Ecclesia** one by one, their order decided by lot. In an adjoining room, a selected group of **Spartiates** could not see what was happening, but could still hear the cheers for each candidate. They decided which candidate had received the loudest cheers, and he was elected to the **Gerousia**.

The Ecclesia: this assembly (which has sometimes been known as the **Apella**) was open to all male citizens over the age of 30. They met monthly under the chairmanship of the **ephors**. They could not discuss or amend proposals made by the **Gerousia**: they had to listen to the views of the **ephors** and/or kings and then vote for or against them. As we have seen, if the **Gerousia** didn't like the verdict of the **Ecclesia**, it could withdraw the proposal. The most important topics they could vote on were: 1. the election of the **Gerousia** and **ephors**; 2. questions of war and peace; 3. foreign policy and the signing of treaties.

Pros and cons of the constitution

The most important point to make about the constitution is that the vast majority of the Spartan population – women, **perioikoi** and **helots** – had no say whatsoever in government. A further important criticism made by Aristotle, a philosopher who studied political systems, was that the **Gerousia** had too much power, considering that its members were likely to be elderly and perhaps out of touch with Spartan society, or even senile! Others might criticise the fact that the decisions of the **Ecclesia** could be overturned if the **Gerousia** were unhappy with them.

However, it could also be argued that the Spartan constitution was well balanced, since no single body could gain too much power. Aristotle didn't know how to describe it, believing that it had elements of tyranny, monarchy, aristocracy and democracy. Indeed, the fact that any member of the **Ecclesia** was eligible to serve as an **ephor** or on the **Gerousia** gave it an important democratic element.

> 1. Which section of the Spartan government do you think was most powerful?
> 2. How effective do you think that the structure of Spartan government was?

Sparta's foreign relations

Sparta's relations with other cities of the Greek world were often tense and troubled. The city was treated with suspicion outside its borders. While all Greeks respected and feared the Spartans' superb military machine, there were aspects of their society which left them uneasy – we shall soon see the disgust they felt for Sparta's women. Neither did they feel comfortable with the fact that Sparta had enslaved other Greeks – it was one thing to enslave non-Greeks (whom they called barbarians), but enslaving Greeks was unusual and made other Greek peoples fear that they might be next. A further cause of concern was the Spartan education system; many other Greeks thought that it was barbaric to send off young children to a military boarding school at the age of seven; they were also appalled by the lack of intellectual content in the school, which encouraged boys to become great warriors at the expense of reading great writers such as Homer.

In their turn, the Spartans were equally suspicious of the outside world, believing that interference by other Greeks might unsettle the status quo in their territory. For this reason, Lykourgos had apparently banned all foreigners from Sparta and also banned the inhabitants of Spartan territory from travelling beyond its borders.

Spartan women

Spartan women were unique in the Greek world. Whereas women in cities like Athens led sheltered lives at home as housewives, in Sparta the women were a visible and important part of society. Women were important to Spartan society for three fundamental reasons: their ability to give birth to strong, healthy children; the economic role they played managing their husbands' farms; and their role in supporting the ideology of the Spartan warrior state.

Sparta was the only society in ancient Greece which had an education system for girls, which had been devised by Lykourgos. Girls lived at home, but may have been organised into bands, as the boys were. At times they may have exercised with the boys and taken part in gymnastic, musical and choral competitions. Young women typically married at the age of about 18, later than women in other Greek cities. The marriage took place in secret: the bride and her family had a simple private ceremony, then her hair was cut off and she was dressed in male clothes. After dinner, the bridegroom quietly came and had sex with her, but he then hurried back to sleep in his barracks, since a man was not allowed live with his wife until he had reached the age of 30.

Bronze statuette of a Spartan girl running or dancing.

A woman's most important role was to produce healthy sons, who would grow up to be fine warriors: women had not only to produce babies, but healthy ones at that! Child mortality rates were very high in the ancient world, and there were no modern medicines to assist the survival of infants during and after pregnancy. For this reason, Spartan women were required to exercise vigorously. Plutarch tells us that they took part in games such as running, wrestling, javelin, discus and ball games. These activities made women healthier, which in turn lessened their risk of miscarriage, prolonged a woman's childbearing years, and helped the development of a healthy infant in the womb.

Spartan women also had a far more powerful economic role than women in any other Greek city. Women did not do housework, spinning or weaving – this was seen to be beneath their dignity and was the duty of helots, whom they supervised. Instead, since Spartiates were forbidden from doing any other

Externally Assessed Units

work than soldiering, it was left to their wives to manage their farming estates. A woman had to ensure that the family had enough food and that her husband provided their monthly ration of food for their **syssition**. Women could also own and inherit property in Sparta (in stark contrast to women elsewhere in the Greek world) and wealthy heiresses were highly prized.

Spartan women were also very important for propaganda purposes. A typical Spartan woman seems to have been a very tough character, who was ready to send her son off to the **Agoge** at the age of seven so that he would grow up to be a brave and strong fighter. Women were fanatical believers in their society – when Spartans went off to war, their womenfolk apparently said goodbye to them with the words 'either with your shield or on it' – meaning that they should either come back victorious or dead!

Spartan women were a source of scandal in the rest of the Greek world. Other Greeks would also have been shocked by the degree of economic power they had in society, while Aristotle probably spoke for many when he claimed that Spartan men were 'ruled by their wives' – he believed them to be far too bossy. Greeks may also have thought of them as bad mothers because they were prepared to send their sons away from home for good at the age of seven.

It seems that adultery was sometimes encouraged in Sparta. If an older Spartan felt that a younger warrior had a better chance of getting his wife pregnant, he could allow that man to sleep with her. This practice appalled other Greeks, who thought that Spartan women were sexually promiscuous. Their anger was also fuelled by the fact that Spartan women were allowed to socialise and exercise with their menfolk, and to visit public places unescorted, something which was unheard of in a city such as Athens. Spartan women were also infamous for wearing short skirts and revealing clothing, so that some Greeks nicknamed them 'thigh-flashers'.

> **What do you admire about Spartan women? Why do you think that they were so important in Spartan society?**

1.6 Pompeii

In late August 79 AD, the town of Pompeii was destroyed in a cataclysmic volcanic eruption. Hundreds of people were killed and the city was submerged in a sea of lava and ash. It was one of the greatest natural disasters in Roman history. Yet, ironically, this destruction was a great gift for later historians. For the way in which Pompeii (and the nearby city of Herculaneum) was buried has meant that a day in history has been frozen in time. Pompeii provides us with the most detailed example of everyday life in the ancient world and a huge amount of our knowledge of Roman society comes from this one site.

Settlement

Pompeii did not become a 'Roman' town until relatively late in its history. It was probably founded by people who lived in the south of Italy in about the 8th century BC, long before the Romans conquered this area. It is also clear that the city was heavily influenced by the many Greek cities which existed in Southern Italy and Sicily. By the 6th century, the settlement had developed a city wall, which was to remain the extent of the city until it was destroyed. Although it was allied to Rome for many years, it was not until the 1st century BC that the Romans took full control of the town. There are some obvious reasons why the site of Pompeii was so appealing to settlers:

- It was built on a **lava spur** created by an earlier eruption of Vesuvius hundreds of years before. This gave the south–west side of the city an excellent natural defence.
- It was next to the **River Sarno**, which was navigable and led inland to other parts of the region, so that Pompeii had control of the traffic up and down the river. The river also provided natural irrigation for the fields nearby, contributing to the fertile environment.
- Pompeii was a harbour town on the Bay of Naples, which gave good access for **trade**. The city was a stopping point on the main north–south trade route between Rome and other parts of the Mediterranean.
- Like all volcanic regions, the slopes of Mt Vesuvius were **richly fertile**. They provided an ideal soil for grape vines, olive trees, grain and fruit trees. Moreover, the woods were also a source of wild animals, fruit, honey, herbs, and wood.

Externally Assessed Units

> What natural advantages caused the area in which you live to be settled?

The destruction

The earthquake of 62 AD

Mt Vesuvius lies in a chain of volcanoes which reaches from the north of Rome in Italy to Mt Etna in Sicily. However, Pompeians seem to have had little idea that the mountain beside their town was volcanic. Despite this, the area was still prone to seismic activity, most notably when a devastating earthquake struck the region in 62 AD. When Vesuvius erupted in 79 AD the town was still recovering from what they considered to be their terrible natural disaster – little did they know what was to come.

Houses and temples had collapsed and people lay buried beneath the rubble. In the aftermath of the event, the Pompeians took the opportunity to improve on what had been there before. In particular, old houses were replaced with newer, more splendid constructions. In some areas, whole blocks of housing were cleared to make room for a large house. The busiest area was the forum, which was given a make-over. However, it was a long process and the town resembled one large building site in the years up to the eruption.

The eruption

Vesuvius erupted on 24th August 79 AD for the first time in over 700 years. In the days and weeks beforehand, there were some warning signs of what was to come: several small earthquakes shook the area, wells dried up and springs stopped flowing, dogs howled and birds were strangely silent. Yet Pompeians ignored the rumblings under their feet and the strange behaviour of their pets.

The eruption started in the middle of the day on the 24th and lasted for about 18 hours, progressing through various stages. Pompeii happened to be down-wind of the volcano on that day, and so volcanic debris was blown over the town. This mainly consisted of pumice and fragments of rock, which started a slow build-up in the town; after a few hours, buildings started to collapse under the weight.

Archaeologists have discovered some bodies of people who were killed at this stage of the eruption either by the collapse of buildings or by being hit directly by falling rocks. However, Pompeians would have had plenty of time to evacuate the town, and so those who stayed behind (only a small minority of the population) probably chose to do so. The final destruction came early the following morning, when one side of the volcano collapsed, triggering a series of 'pyroclastic surges' – flows and surges of hot ash and gases (between 100 and 400 degrees centigrade) that swept over Pompeii and buried it. All those left in the town were killed by this final phase, either by suffocation from poisonous gases, or by thermal shock.

The two Plinys

We are very fortunate that the eruption in 79 AD was the first ever volcanic eruption to be recorded in writing by an eye-witness. Pliny 'the Younger' was a 17 year old boy staying with his uncle, Pliny 'the Elder', who was a remarkable man – both a brilliant natural historian and an admiral in the Roman navy. The younger Pliny wrote two letters to the historian Tacitus telling him what he saw of the eruption from his uncle's house on the north side of the Bay of Naples. These letters also tell of his uncle's brave attempt to sail to the rescue of people trapped on the shore and his death from suffocation by the poisonous fumes from the volcano. The younger Pliny only narrowly avoided death himself, but he went on to become a prominent Roman citizen who became a provincial governor.

Rediscovery

Pompeii lay hidden for centuries until it was rediscovered in the middle of the 18th century. However, the earliest excavators were very careless, often doing great damage to buildings, while valuable artefacts were removed for private collectors. It wasn't until the middle of the 19th century that a proper approach to the excavations was developed. The key figure in this movement was **Giuseppe Fiorelli**, an Italian who brought a far more scientific approach to the excavation of Pompeii.

Fiorelli is most famous for his plastercasts, produced by a process which was named after him: **Fiorelli's Process**. He realised that where a corpse had been buried in ash, it had rotted over time and a cavity remained. Whenever an excavator discovered a cavity, plaster of Paris was poured in and left to harden. The ash around the plaster was then carefully removed, so that a plaster

Externally Assessed Units

replica of a person at the moment of death remained. This process gave information about how people had died in the eruption, what they were doing in their final moments, and what sort of clothing they wore. Fiorelli's Process has also been used to get plastercasts of other organic material such as wooden shutters, doors, furniture, and even root cavities, informing us what plants people grew in their gardens.

Fiorelli was also responsible for a number of other improvements in the excavations:

- **Numbering**. He introduced a system of triple numbering: the town was divided into nine regions, the blocks in each region were in turn numbered, and then individual buildings in each block were numbered.
- **Records**. He also introduced a *Journal of Excavations* in which detailed notes were kept of all the finds. If items were removed, they were taken to the Naples Archaeological Museum, while replicas were left in their place (e.g. the faun in the House of the Faun). Fiorelli banned the removal of items for private collections.
- **Protection**. He built roofs over excavated buildings in order to protect them from the sun and rain; he also cleared away the mounds of waste which were littered around the Pompeii site.

> 1. Imagine you are in Pompeii when Vesuvius erupts. Write an account of what you see and what you do.
> 2. How did Fiorelli's methods enable us to learn more about Pompeii?

The forum

The heart of Pompeii was its forum, situated in the south-west of the town near the gate which led to the harbour. It had the feel of a modern city centre. At its heart was a paved open area in which much of the city's life took place: politicians came to speak and win influence, while many people just met socially; the forum was lined with statues of important public figures in the town and the wider Roman Empire. The whole area was a pedestrian precinct, with blocking stones preventing access for vehicles from adjoining streets.

1.6 Pompeii

Around the forum lay the town's grandest buildings, none more so than the imposing Temple of Jupiter to the north, which was flanked on either side by a ceremonial arch. Skirting the rest of the forum ran a double colonnade, part of which is still in place today. In the porticoes beyond the colonnade traders set up their stalls during the day so that the forum became a live market. The buildings which lay beyond the porticoes can be categorised as religious, commercial or political.

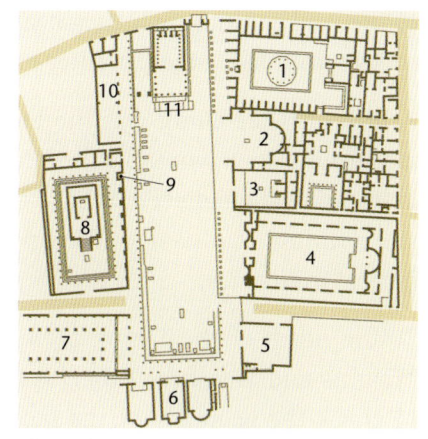

Plan of the forum, Pompeii.

Religious buildings

The forum was the religious heart of the Pompeii and contained four of the town's main temples. To the north was the **Temple of Jupiter** [11], the most important temple in the city, which was also dedicated to Juno and Minerva. It was the most prominent building in the forum and symbolised the power of Roman state religion. To the west was the **Temple of Apollo** [8], one of the earliest temples of the town, dating to the 6th century BC; the worship of Apollo perhaps suggests early Greek influence on Pompeii. Inside the sanctuary, two bronze statues were found – one of Apollo with his bow and the other of his sister, Diana.

To the east side of the forum were the **Temple of the Emperor** [3] and the **Temple of the Public Lares** [2]. The former was where Pompeians worshipped the Roman emperor (who was Vespasian in 79 AD), since emperors were worshipped as gods. The latter is thought to be where people worshipped their ancestors, the protective spirits (or 'Lares') of the town.

Commercial buildings

The forum was also the business centre of Pompeii, containing buildings concerned with various trades and industries. To the north-east was the **Macellum** [1], a covered market selling meat and fish. In the centre was an open area with a circular building holding a pool of water with fish for sale. Around the edge of the Macellum, both inside and outside, were shops; some of the wall paintings which still survive indicate what goods were sold there – they include fish, bread, poultry and wine.

A little further along was the **Eumachia Building** [4], so called because it was funded by a woman called Eumachia, a wealthy Pompeian priestess. It is traditionally believed to have been a guildhall for the fullers of Pompeii, since fulling (cloth-manufacturing) may well have been one of the city's largest industries.

To the north of the Temple of Apollo were two other commercial sites: the **Weights and Measures Table** [9] and the **Granary** [10]. The former was used to check the accuracy of the measures of the forum traders. The table has nine holes, each one equal to a specific measure and with a mini trapdoor at the base. When the hole was filled to the brim, the trapdoor was released and the exact amount contained fell into a pot below. As its name suggests, the Granary was used to store grain and cereal to be sold in the forum.

Political buildings

At the south end of the forum were five buildings which formed the heart of the government of Pompeii. These consisted of three municipal offices for the town councillors, the **Basilica** [7] – a law court and business centre – and the **Comitium** [5], a polling station where the town's elections were held.

Pompeii's political system was based on the system of government at Rome. The two most important magistrates were the **duovirs**, who made legal decisions, managed public funds and oversaw meetings of the town council. Below them were two further magistrates, the **aediles**, who were responsible for more menial administration, such as road maintenance, the supervision of markets and the upkeep of public temples. Each pair of magistrates was based in one of the municipal offices. The third municipal office was the **Curia** [6], the meeting place of the town council, which consisted of about 100 members known as **decurions**, mostly former **aediles** or **duovirs**. Elections for the four senior positions were held annually in the Comitium.

The Basilica was one of the most important public buildings in Pompeii, serving as a law court and a centre for business and financial transactions. At the far end of the building there was a raised platform, which was probably used for judges in trials or auctioneers at auctions.

Politics in Pompeii

The evidence from Pompeii suggests that the annual elections were hard fought affairs. On many outside walls of buildings painted slogans and graffiti can still be seen advertising a particular candidate for election. The following is typical:

> *I ask you to elect as aedile for taking care of sacred and public buildings Lucius Popidius Amplitus, a fine young man worthy of public office.*

Many of these advertisements suggest that traders formed guilds (trade unions) which backed candidates favourable to them:

> *All the fruit-sellers with Helvius Vestalis call for Marconius Holconius Priscus as duovir for lawsuits.*

1. How does Pompeii's forum compare to a modern town centre?
2. Imagine you pay a visit to Pompeii's forum. Describe some of the people you meet there.

Private houses

The typical design of a wealthy Roman town house (known in Latin as a **domus**) was built around three important uses of space: the **atrium**, **tablinum** and **peristylium**, which followed one behind the other. Entrance into a house was via a large door and narrow entrance way. Alongside this on the outside of the house were typically shops giving onto the street. The house's owners could make money by renting out these shops to traders.

The **atrium** was the main entrance room of the house, into which the visitor would first arrive, and so had to be visually impressive. It would have a hole in its roof from which water would fall into a well (**impluvium**) in the centre of the room. In this way the household could store some water. On either side of the **atrium** would typically be small bedrooms, while beyond it was the **tablinum**, the main study or office of the master of the house. Its significance can be seen from the fact that it was the central room in the whole house. Behind the **tablinum** was the **peristylium**, a colonnaded garden which was a private area for the family; only close family friends would be invited through here.

Externally Assessed Units

Of the rooms around the **peristylium**, at least one would be a dining room, while there were usually also further bedrooms and a kitchen. Many houses also had an upstairs area, but little evidence of these has remained after the eruption.

The furniture in a house was usually sparing, with beds and dining couches the main items. However, wealthier houses were often decorated in two different artistic mediums: the mosaic and the wall painting, both of which typically depicted stories from history or mythology.

The House of the Vettii

This house is named after the two **Vettii** brothers, who lived there at the time of the eruption. They were freedmen who seem to have acquired great wealth; something indicated by the way that they had rebuilt the house after the earthquake. On its outside, there are no shops adjoining its high walls, nor did the house have a **tablinum**. Both of these facts suggest that the brothers were so wealthy that they didn't need to earn money from **clients**. The house's entrance is famous for its painting of the god Priapus weighing his phallus; this was a common image in Pompeii to symbolise wealth and prosperity.

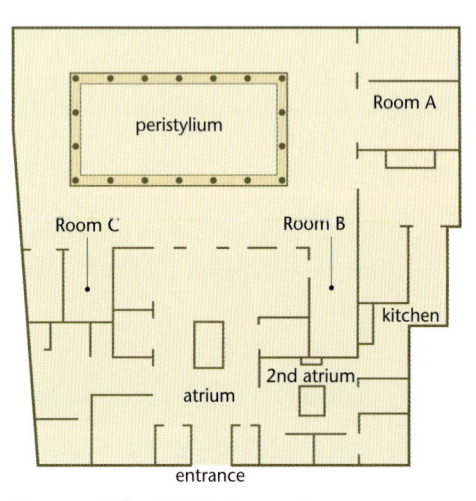

House of the Vettii, Pompeii.

One of the house's distinctive features was that it had two **atria**. In the first **atrium** were found two large bronze chests, used to store the wealth of the household. Next to the second **atrium** was a kitchen and one of the house's two sets of service quarters. One of the rooms here contains a set of erotic paintings. The other set of service quarters is on the other side of the main **atrium**; this area may well have contained a stable for horses.

The focal point of the house was its **peristylium**, whose garden had a number of running fountains (the house had its own water supply) as well as statues made of bronze or marble. The garden was surrounded by the main receptions rooms: it was rare for a Roman house to base itself around its garden in this way.

1.6 Pompeii

Three of the five reception rooms were decorated with beautiful wall paintings depicting scenes from Greek mythology:

- **Room A** contains the Cupids' Frieze, which portrays various Cupids engaged in commercial activities, such as making perfume and garlands, working metal and baking bread.
- **Room B** is most famous for its painting of the punishment of Ixion for trying to rape Hera. He was tied to an ever-spinning wheel.
- **Room C** has three paintings, the most notable of which is the depiction of Pentheus being torn apart by the Bacchae.

As with any house, this one tells us a good deal about its owners, even from a distance of two thousand years. The Vettii brothers, as freed slaves who had made a lot of money, were naturally keen to show off all the riches they had amassed. The Priapus painting and the bronze chests are powerful statements of this wealth. In addition, the brothers were presumably keen entertainers since they had so many reception rooms. Their display of Greek art and mythology also suggests that they were trying to present themselves as educated and refined, since knowledge of Greek culture was considered to be essential for a well-educated Roman.

The House of the Faun

This is one of the largest houses in Pompeii, occupying the length of a whole block. It is distinctive for having **two atria**, each of which could be entered from a front door on the street. However, one was more important than the other – the 'main atrium', which led into the **tablinum**, was where clients and business contacts

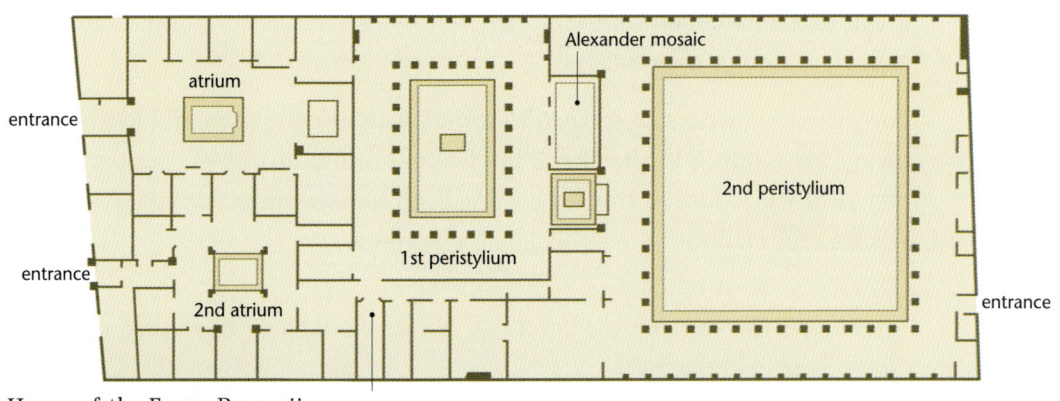

House of the Faun, Pompeii.

113

Externally Assessed Units

would be received; it was therefore designed to create a powerful impression. The house also takes its name from the statuette of a dancing faun found in the **impluvium** of this main **atrium**. The second **atrium** was a more intimate place and was perhaps used by family members or any friends staying with the family.

The house had other important features, which can be summarised as follows:

- Because of its size, it was able to accommodate not one but two **peristylia**, which were separated by a summer room. On the floor of this summer room was the house's grandest work of art – a huge mosaic of a battle between Alexander the Great and the Persian emperor Darius when Alexander was leading his Greek soldiers on a conquest of the Persian Empire.
- Leading off from the second atrium was a service quarters for slaves. This led into the larger **peristylium**, which itself had a door onto the street at the back of the house. This meant that slaves and traders could enter and work in the house without disturbing their master.
- The house had its own water supply and bathing room, which was equipped with a **hypocaust** (see page 117). Only the very wealthy could afford to have a bath complex at home.
- In addition to the statuette of the dancing faun and the Alexander mosaic, the house contained many other impressive works of art, including mosaics depicting sea creatures, scenes on the river Nile, and a cat carrying a dead bird in its mouth.

It is not clear who owned the House of the Faun at the time of the eruption. However, the house does suggest something about the owners' personalities. They clearly enjoyed entertaining, and had the second **atrium** for the use of private guests. In addition to this, the house also had four dining rooms, one for each season of the year.

Moreover, the owners seem keen to show off their education and learning by having art relating to the Greek intellectual and cultural world, just as the owners of the House of the Vettii were. Both houses emphasise the respect in which Greek civilisation was held by the Romans.

> Which of the two houses described above would you have preferred to have lived in and why?

Inns and thermopolia

Since Pompeii was a town which thrived on trade with many other parts of the Roman Empire, it was visited by many traders and merchants. These visitors provided an industry for the town in themselves, as Pompeii needed bars and inns in order to cater for them. These came in different shapes and sizes, but the most common type sold hot food and wine and was known as a **thermopolium**. Some **thermopolia** were simply snack-bars, while others doubled up as inns for travellers. In addition, there is evidence of larger inns where there are even stables to tether horses. Bars and inns have been found all over Pompeii, but were particularly common near to the main gates and busiest streets. They were also popular because they gave the poor an opportunity to eat hot food if they did not have proper cooking facilities at home.

The Thermopolium of Asellina

The best preserved **thermopolium** in Pompeii is named after Asellina, who is believed to have been a waitress who worked there. It was located on Pompeii's main shopping street and had rooms for rent upstairs. It had an open front giving out onto the street; there was a counter giving out onto the street on one side; built into it were storage jars where different foods were kept. There was also room for seats and tables, although most customers probably chose to 'take-away' their purchases from the front counter. The bar is also famous for its painted shrine on the back wall. On the far left is depicted Mercury, who was the god responsible for traders, while at the other end is Bacchus, the Roman god of wine. The owners of the bar clearly hoped that both these gods would bless their business.

A bar such as this one was not just a place for people to buy food. As with a modern pub or bar today, it was a place for friends to socialise and play games. Wall paintings in **thermopolia** show people gambling, drinking, fighting and kissing. Dice have also been found in some bars.

Food and drink

Many different types of food have been discovered in the **thermopolia**, including bread, walnuts, almonds, dates, figs and olives. Many animal bones, fish bones and shellfish also have been uncovered, suggesting that the locals had a

Externally Assessed Units

varied diet. Wine was the drink of choice, and this could be produced locally or imported from different areas of the Mediterranean.

> Why do you think that thermopolia were so popular in Pompeii?

The baths

Bathing was central to life in the Roman world. Only the very wealthiest people could afford to have their own set of baths at home, and so the vast majority kept clean by visiting one of the public bath houses on a daily basis. These bath houses were funded by the government; while this might seem generous, it was in everybody's interest to make sure that people had a basic level of hygiene and so to prevent the spread of disease. Therefore, entrance to the baths was either free or cost very little.

At the time of the eruption, Pompeii had three bath houses (and a fourth was under construction); the oldest and largest of these, now known as the **Stabian Baths**, was located in the heart of the town. Its remains can tell us a great deal about the Roman bathing experience. The baths were divided into two areas – one for women and one for men. A man entered via the main entrance, alongside which there were various shops and bars. He would head to the changing room, the **apodyterium** [2], which had benches and niches for clothes. At this stage, he would get a slave to rub oil all over his body (Romans did not have soap and so used olive oil to clean themselves).

Before bathing a visitor would probably first work up a sweat in the **palaestra** [1], or exercise-ground, where he might lift some weights, fence with a wooden sword or throw and catch balls. He could also have a dip in the swimming pool next to the **palaestra**. Then he would head into the suite of baths. There were three main rooms:

- He first headed to the **tepidarium** [3], which was a warm room where he could sit on a bench and gradually get used to the heat.
- He then moved into the hottest room the **caldarium** [4], where he could either sit in a hot bath or just sit on a bench in the steam. The room also contained a basin providing cold water if he wanted to cool his face. Before

1.6 Pompeii

he moved out of this room, he would get a slave to rub off the oil from his body using a curved metal scraper known as a **strigil**.
- The final stage of the bathing was the **frigidarium** [5], a much cooler room with a cold plunge pool. He would jump into this pool to wash himself clean and allow the pores of his skin to close.

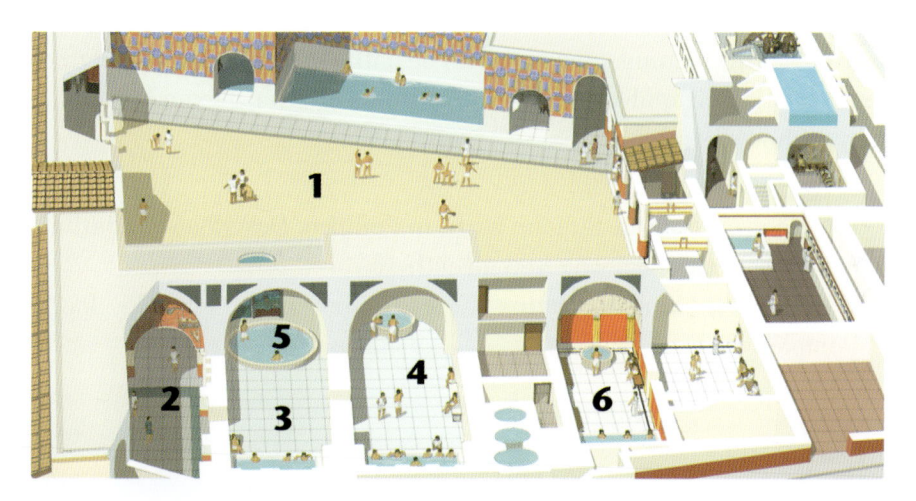

The Stabian Baths, Pompeii.

The Stabian Baths also had a separate bathing area for women [6], who entered by an entrance at the back of the complex. Their area had no **frigidarium**, but there was a cold bath in the changing room. They were not allowed to bath with the men, nor could they use the **palaestra** or the swimming pool.

The baths were heated by an underground heating system known as a **hypocaust**. In fact, the Stabian Baths have the earliest example of a **hypocaust** system in the Roman world. The floor in the warmer rooms was supported by pillars. To the side, slaves would stoke a furnace, from which hot air would pass under the floor and heat it up. Some baths, including those at Pompeii, also had hollow walls to enable them to be heated up by the rising of the hot air.

The importance of the baths

The baths were not simply a place where people went to get clean. They were a very important social and business meeting place. In the pattern of the Roman day, people went to work in the morning and then to the baths in the afternoon. Roman businessmen did not normally have offices, and so many would

Externally Assessed Units

conduct business meetings in the baths. It was a place to make contacts and show off one's power – many rich men made a point of being escorted to the baths by as many slaves as possible to display their wealth and power.

The baths were also a place to socialise and so can really be compared to a sports centre or gym today. People would often meet there before going off to a friend's house for dinner – the bathing experience was often a way of getting ready for an evening engagement. The baths kept Romans healthy, acted as a social club and enabled them to do business. It is hard to imagine Roman society without them.

1. Imagine you visit the Stabian baths in Pompeii. Describe your bathing experience and the people you meet there.
2. Why do you think the baths were so important to everyday life in Pompeii?

The theatre

Pompeii had its very own theatre district with two theatres. The smaller of the two was probably used only for recitals of poetry or music, while plays were put on in the larger theatre, which had a capacity of about 5,000.

Roman comedy

Drama came to the Romans from the Greek world. The Romans were particularly keen on comedy, and their most famous comic playwright was **Plautus**. His plays typically contain a strong element of farce and slapstick, with actors playing stock characters from everyday Roman life.

Most plots centre on the tricks of a resourceful slave to help the love affair of his young master who is being threatened by a rival or a strict father. The girl he has fallen for might be a slave-girl or prostitute who is eventually discovered to be free-born, since she has been kidnapped in childhood. Her recognition would form the climax of the play, after which she would be eligible to marry her lover. Typical stock characters would be a boastful soldier, a sponger and a cook.

As in ancient Greece, actors wore masks, which were usually caricatures of the characters being portrayed. Comic masks had great grinning mouths; a male character was portrayed with a brown mask, a female with a white one. The masks also allowed actors to play a variety of roles. Costumes also gave a clear indication of the character on stage. For example, a white costume was used for an old man, a multi-coloured one for a youth; yellow was used for a prostitute, purple for the rich and red for the poor. A slave wore a short tunic and a soldier wore a cloak.

The theatre

The large theatre was built into a natural hillside at the southern end of the town. The seating area was semi-circular. The most important men in Pompeii, such as the **decurions**, sat in the front rows; behind them sat the rest of the audience. There were a number of aisles running up the seating area, which made it easy for everyone to get to and from their seats. The seats themselves were not wide – one estimate suggests that each person filled a width of about 40cm. However, the audience were provided with some comfort by a huge awning which provided shade from the sun. Moreover, during intervals the audience was sometimes sprayed with scented water to keep them cool.

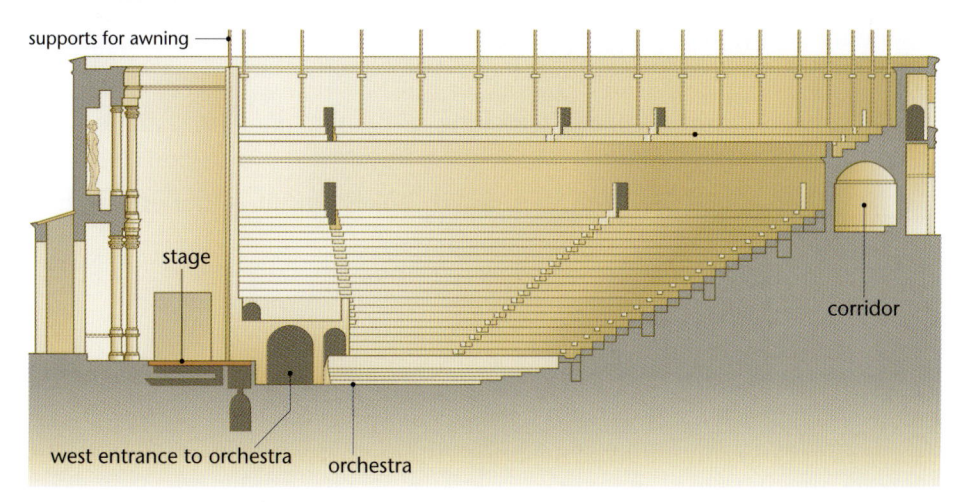

Plan of the theatre, Pompeii.

Of the acting area itself, the main actors performed on the stage. However, in front of them and almost amongst the audience was the orchestra, where musicians would perform between scenes and during the play to add atmosphere to the play. As today, the stage was given scenery to create a setting; scenes painted would obviously depend on the plot, but for comic plays there would usually be a street-scene from everyday life, with private buildings, balconies and windows painted in. A door could also be decorated to represent the entrance to a house, while colonnades and temple facades might also create the impression of public spaces.

The audience

Roman audiences were very vocal in expressing their views. Sources suggest that they soon became bored if they couldn't follow the plot or, on the other hand, if it was too similar to plays they had seen before. If an actor sang out of tune or mispronounced his lines then he could be insulted, hissed at, or booed off stage. However, if the audience were pleased with what they saw, they would clap and cheer wildly.

Famous actors could be hero worshipped in Pompeii. One actor called Paris is the subject of a number of graffiti, including 'Paris, pearl of the stage' and 'Paris sweet darling', while he even had a fan club which signed itself 'the comrades of Paris'. In spite of this, however, most actors were looked down on in Roman society and often regarded in the same light as prostitutes.

> 1. How would you compare watching a Roman play to watching a play today?
> 2. To what extent do comedies today poke fun at situations from everyday life?

The amphitheatre

Pompeii's amphitheatre was located in the south-east corner of the town, with a large exercise ground situated next to it. Although its capacity of 15,000 was much smaller than that of the Colosseum in Rome, it was still a huge arena for a moderately sized town. Gladiators were clearly important to the Pompeians – at the other end of the town there was even a special barracks where gladiators lived and trained.

1.6 Pompeii

The evidence indicates that shows put on there were much the same as those of the Colosseum (see page 43); most common were gladiatorial fights and wild beast hunts. As in Rome, games were paid for by a sponsor – a wealthy public figure who wished to gain popularity. In the lead-up to his games, he would pay for advertisements to be painted on the walls of the main streets, making sure that everyone knew who was providing the games, as these words from a surviving poster indicate:

> *Alleius Nigidius Maius ... is providing thirty pairs of gladiators and their substitutes; they will fight at Pompeii on 24, 25 and 26 November. There will be a hunt. Long live Maius.*

The riot

One of the few occasions when Pompeii is mentioned by ancient historians was after a riot in its amphitheatre in 59 AD. The historian Tacitus recounts how Pompeian spectators started to engage in a slanging match with other spectators who had come from the nearby town of Nuceria. Things soon became violent – at first stones were thrown, then swords were drawn and a full-scale fight broke out; a famous wall painting in a Pompeian house depicts the fighting in and around the arena. By the end, many were killed and Tacitus comments that 'the people of Pompeii came off best'.

The emperor at the time, Nero, was concerned by news of unrest between two provincial towns. He ordered the Senate to hold an investigation, after which Pompeii was banned from holding games in its amphitheatre for ten years. In addition, the sponsor of the games was sent into exile.

> **How similar were shows in Pompeii's ampitheatre to sporting events today?**

1.7 Tackling the written examination

This chapter aims to show you the types of questions you are likely to get in the written examination, and to give you some advice on how to deal with them.

The examination

All the questions are designed to test three things:

1. **Factual Knowledge** (35% of the marks): Do you have a good range of knowledge, particularly the key facts associated with the areas of the options that you have studied? As well as gaining you marks, having a good factual knowledge of the topics will enable you to deal in a thorough way with the other types of question you will meet.
2. **Understanding** (30% of the marks): Do you appreciate the way people lived, why they behaved in certain ways and what was important to them? Do you understand how different aspects of each option relate to each other and also the various terms that you find in each option? This should become clearer when looking at examples of actual questions.
3. **Interpretation/Evaluation (analysis)** (35% of the marks): Can you make observations about what the sources tell us? Can you explain why certain things were important to the people of ancient Rome/Greece? Can you explain what attitudes the ancients took to different aspects of their culture and why they behaved the way they did? Can you relate the source material to what you know about ancient society? Again this should become clearer when looking at examples of actual questions.

How does the written examination do this?

There are three clear parts to the Classical Civilisation GCSE. All students attempt two:

- Foundation Tier: students attempt Part 1 (Multiple Choice Section) and Part 2 (Source Based Questions).
- Higher Tier: students attempt Part 2 (Source Based Questions) and Part 3 (Essay Questions).

1.7 Tackling the written examination

Part 1: Multiple Choice Questions

Whether you are a foundation tier candidate or not, it is worth your while looking at how this section works. Use some of the styles of question to help you revise in line with the three main aspects of factual knowledge, understanding and interpretation/evaluation.

This section is not a one-word answer section. You will be asked to match information, put information in sequence or assess the truth or relevance of information, as well as to identify key facts.

A sound factual knowledge is vital for all sections of the multiple choice section.

One way basic factual knowledge will be tested is by asking you to choose the correct piece of information from a list. You may have to complete a sentence, for example:

(b)	Laps in the Circus Maximus were counted using	A… horses	
		B… dolphins	
		C… counters	
		D… eagles	

It may be tested by matching different bits of information, for example:

Look at the table below, and the list of words on page 124. Match the god with their area of responsibility and what symbol they are typically represented with.

God	Responsibility	Symbol
Example: Neptune	*Sea*	*Trident*
Mercury		
Ceres		
Vesta		

Externally Assessed Units

Responsibility
Fertility
Messenger
Hearth
Sea

Symbol
Trident
Fire
Winged sandals
Crops

Each time you will be given an example to show you how to answer the question.

Your understanding of a particular topic may be tested by asking you to choose statements which relate to a particular topic, for example:

Apollo was a particularly **important** god because

A he was often portrayed as a hunter ☐

B he could help people look into the future ☐

C he was a very handsome god ☐

D he had a sister who was also a goddess ☐

Notice here that all the statements are true of Apollo but we are looking for the key element of **importance**. Only by reading this type of question carefully can you identify the answer that fits in with what is required.

You may be asked to choose more than one true statement from a list, for example:

Choose **three** of the following sentences which apply to the sentence below.

The riot in the Amphitheatre in 59 AD was a significant event to Pompeii because

(i) The emperor banned games for ten years.

(ii) Nobody wanted to put on games after that as the Pompeians were so ashamed.

1.7 Tackling the written examination

> (iii) So many Pompeians were killed by their neighbours from Nuceria.
> (iv) Many gladiators escaped and ran riot through the streets.
> (v) Gladiatorial supporters from other towns came to challenge the Pompeians, so Pompeii was far less safe.
> (vi) Many politicians lost the chance to gain the support of the people.

Again, notice that you are being asked about your understanding of the consequences of the riot, not the factual details.

If you know your facts, and if you understand their significance, then you are in a position to **interpret and evaluate**. Multiple choice questions which ask you to do this will be in various forms.

They may be 'true or false' questions, for example:

> **Education of Boys and Girls in Athens**
>
> Some of the following statements are true and some are false. Tick the 'true' box if the statement is true. Tick the 'false' box if it is not.
>
> | | True | False |
> |---|---|---|
> | (a) Girls were educated by their fathers. | ☐ | ☐ |
> | (b) Girls needed to be educated for a role in politics. | ☐ | ☐ |
> | (c) Exercise was an important part of a boy's education. | ☐ | ☐ |
> | (d) Learning to weave was an important part of a girl's education. | ☐ | ☐ |
> | (e) Boys and girls were taught together. | ☐ | ☐ |

Here the evaluation comes about by using the **knowledge** that you have about education in ancient Athens, the **understanding** you have of what it was aimed to achieve and how it worked; so that you can evaluate the truth of the statements that you have been given.

Externally Assessed Units

A very important skill which will also test your evaluation will be to make sure you can list events in the right order. This will show that you can put together a complete picture of an event by looking at its various parts.

An example might be the sequence of a Greek or Roman sacrifice, worded in the following way:

A Roman sacrifice

Put the following in the order in which they happened using the numbers 2 to 6. Number 1 has been provided.

worshipper goes to buy an animal	1
entrails examined to see if animal healthy	☐
strike with hammer	☐
procession	☐
dress in ribbons	☐
pluck lock of hair	☐

Remember that at some stage you may be asked about the significance or importance of any or all of these aspects.

Remember that the multiple choice section is not intended to trick you in any way or ask for obscure details. The factual knowledge required will be relatively basic in relation to the topic areas. Nevertheless there will be a need for you to think about the facts and, just as importantly, make sure you have read the question carefully.

Part 2: Source-based questions

All students who enter for Classical Civilisation will have to attempt one of three source-based questions. (See also the guidance about sources on pages 8–9 above.)

1.7 Tackling the written examination

Once again the focus is on testing your factual knowledge, your understanding of the classical world and your ability to interpret/evaluate aspects of it.

The three demands will be clearly defined in the questions. Usually the evaluation is tested by your ability to look at and interpret the source material. Look at the example of a Pompeii question below.

---

1 Study the picture below and then answer **all** the questions that follow.

(a) How is this theatre typical of a Roman theatre? [5]

(b) Explain how comfortable a Roman audience was when watching a play. [5]

(c) Explain why Roman comedies were entertaining for a lower class Roman audience. [5]

[Total: 15]

The first question asks you to identify key features of this theatre which you would expect to find in other theatres. This is interpretation of the source. Again, if you are practised in looking at sources you have not seen before, you will be comfortable in looking for typical features of them.

127

Externally Assessed Units

The second question asks you to show your factual knowledge of the theatre and aspects of comfort. You need to consider relevant facts; factual knowledge questions will not ask you just to write down everything you know. It's about choosing some facts which are relevant to the question and dismissing others.

The third question tests your understanding of the role of comedies in the lives of the audience who watched them. This is where we have to show understanding of the audience of the time and try to avoid a modern viewpoint.

When you are given a written source, the questions are intended to get you thinking about the subject matter. Look at the example below.

---

1 The passage below refers to the helots in Sparta.

Read the passage and then answer **all** the questions that follow.

The Spartans made a proclamation to them to choose any who claimed that they had proved themselves excellent fighters for Sparta during wartime. The Spartans then said that they would set them free. They did this as a test, for they believed that those who thought themselves worthy of being set free would be the ones most likely to attack the Spartans.

[THUCYDIDES]

(a) Describe how and why the Spartans took over the helots' land. [5]

(b) Explain how and why the Spartans treated the helots badly. [5]

(c) Can the Spartans' treatment of this class of society be justified? Explain your opinions. [5]

[Total: 15]

1.7 Tackling the written examination

The first question asks you to show your factual knowledge of Spartan history. The second question tests your understanding of what motivated the Spartans to behave the way they did. The third question asks you to make judgements about Sparta in the context of Spartan society; this is a form of evaluation.

Here are some questions you might like to consider. They are based upon the study of Athens and Rome but the topic does not really matter. The skill is to identify what the question is aiming to test. Is it factual knowledge, understanding or evaluation? You might like to discuss these questions with others and see if you agree.

> 1. Do you think an Athenian boy's education prepared him for later life?
> 2. Describe the basic design of an Athenian house.
> 3. Give details of how the paterfamilias was involved in religion.
> 4. Explain why some slaves were more expensive than others.
> 5. Describe the main stages of a sacrifice in ancient Athens/Rome.
> 6. Explain why the Greeks made many of their temples impressive.
> 7. Was the worship of Athene the only purpose of the Great Panathenaia?
> 8. Explain why the shows in the Colosseum appealed to the Roman audience.
> 9. Explain one reason why religious festivals were important to Rome.
> 10. Did religion dominate family life in ancient Rome?
> 11. Who stood to gain the most from a marriage in Roman times, the husband or the wife?
> 12. Why did wealthy Athenians not spend a great deal on making their houses look spectacular?

Key points

- **Factual knowledge** questions will usually ask you to select relevant facts NOT just give a shopping list of everything you know about a subject.
- **Understanding** means you know why people behaved the way they did in the context of their own society.
- **Evaluation** tends to require you to make judgements as to likely effects or consequences of things being the way they were.

Externally Assessed Units

> **TAKING IT FURTHER**
>
> 1. Find a photograph or other piece of source material based upon a topic you are studying and have studied and see if you can write your own set of three questions testing the three skills.
> 2. Then write a marking scheme to include the kind of answers you would expect to see for each of the questions.
> 3. Pass the test on to another member of the group and see what answers he or she comes up with. Do they match your expectations? If not, why not?

Part 3: Essay questions

Only those of you entering for the higher tier option will be attempting essay questions. These bring together all three of the criteria referred to in the previous section in one piece of continuous writing.

Before looking at these in detail it is worth identifying some key principles which you need to adopt when dealing with this type of question. To some extent, that simply means avoiding some of the pitfalls which prevent people from producing their best in this section of the paper. Usually students read the question properly and understand what it is the examiner is asking them to do. But there can still be a problem, which may arise for one of two reasons:

1. Students have done an essay very similar during their years of study and read the exam question as another way of asking for the answer they have previously prepared.
2. Students lose sight of the focus of the question because they do not go back to what the question asks whilst writing their essays.

These two pitfalls can be avoided by one simple technique: identify in the question (even underline or highlight) the 'buzz-words'. These are the words that direct the way you are to use the factual material and how you should angle your discussion. It is this focus which dictates to you which facts will be relevant and which will not; they will focus you on what you need to show you understand and, just as importantly, they will highlight what evaluation is required.

1.7 Tackling the written examination

Here are some essay questions to compare. They are in pairs. The topic area is the same but the focus is different to a greater or lesser degree. Which words would you highlight in each in order to identify the difference between the two and the direction your discussion should take?

> 1. (a) 'It is difficult to decide if a state sacrifice was designed to please a god or to demonstrate to the public the importance of state religion.'
>   Is this a fair assessment? Explain your opinions.
>   (b) By referring to what took place at a sacrifice in ancient Greece, explain the importance of each stage of the ceremony.

> 2. (a) 'No matter how much historians discuss the importance of the *symposium*, the truth is that it was no more than an excuse for men to party without their wives.'
>   Is this a fair assessment of a *symposium* in ancient Greece?
>   (b) Explain the importance to an Athenian family of a *symposium* in ancient Athens.

> 3. (a) 'Slavery was a cruel institution but necessary for any Roman family.'
>   To what extent is this a fair assessment of slavery in ancient Rome?
>   (b) 'If slavery had not existed, life for a Roman family would have been very different.'
>   Is this a fair assessment?

The factual content is largely the same but the way it will be used will be slightly different for each of the pairs of essays. This is where your understanding and evaluation marks are scored.

The factual content of essays

There are two very important things that you must note:

1. You only include facts that are relevant to the focus of the question ('buzz words')
2. You make the facts valid by including them in a discussion, not writing out what you know about a topic then moving on to give your opinion.

Externally Assessed Units

Look at these extracts from a student essay. The question, based on the Sparta option, is given first.

> 'The reality was that the ephors controlled everything; therefore the other sections of Spartan government were irrelevant.'
>
> Is this an accurate conclusion about the government of Sparta?
>
> Explain your opinions.

EXTRACT 1

The responsibilities of the ephors included supervising the kings and the education system, dealing with foreign ambassadors, acting as judges, declaring war on the helots and choosing the members of the Krypteia. **However, despite this power,** it was the Ecclesia, the assembly of all male Spartans over the age of 30, who elected the ephors and **so one could say the power to elect the people with power was the Ecclesia.** Despite this the Ecclesia's power was also limited because, although they voted for or against proposals, these proposals were drawn up by the Gerousia (Council of Elders aged 60 years and over) and the Ecclesia could not discuss proposals but only vote.

EXTRACT 2

It would perhaps be a fairer analysis to say that although the ephors had arguably the most power in times of peace, this power was only gained by being elected by the Ecclesia once a year and with the cooperation of all the other sections of the government. **This, then, means that the other sections were far from irrelevant** since all sections of their government had a vital role to play in ensuring the smooth running of Sparta.

Notice how the facts are brought into the discussion and made relevant by focusing on the title. The bold areas show how the points are linked together. In the second extract they show how the focus of the question, including words from the actual title, are brought into view.

When you write an essay, get two different coloured highlighter pens. Highlight your discussion in one colour and your facts in another. The final picture

1.7 Tackling the written examination

should show the colours mixed together and alternating. If a large section of your page is one colour you have either become too factual or you are making lots of points but not supporting them with facts. Either way your essay will not hold together as well as it could and should.

Preparing for the written examination

The foundation of your success lies in your factual knowledge and your revision. Revision is far more effective if you have worked out a plan in advance – getting home at night and thinking 'What shall I revise tonight?' is not the way forward and will cost you time, a vital commodity. So, get organised:

- Find somewhere quiet to work, somewhere that you feel comfortable.
- Take frequent breaks; work in short bursts. Every 30 minutes or so, change topic or subject.
- When you're revising, the trick is to be active. That means not simply reading your books/notes and hoping that it will sink in, but actually doing something with the information.
- Prioritise your knowledge.

Here is one way of 'prioritising your knowledge'. For every topic and sub topic think of four key facts that you think you should know. They are gems of knowledge, so turn them into diamonds. For example:

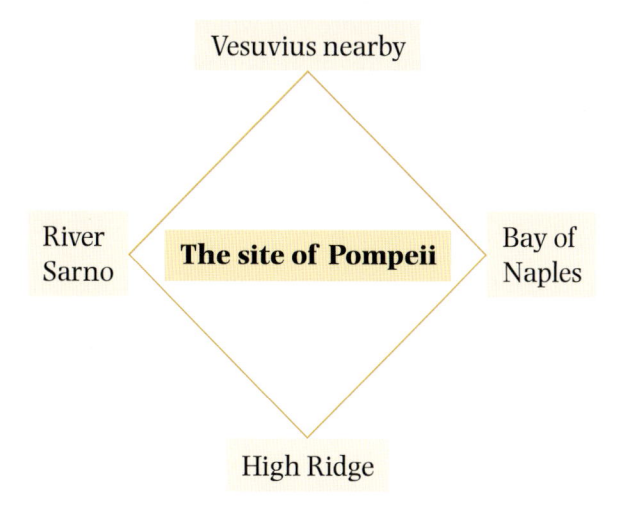

Vesuvius nearby

River Sarno — **The site of Pompeii** — Bay of Naples

High Ridge

Externally Assessed Units

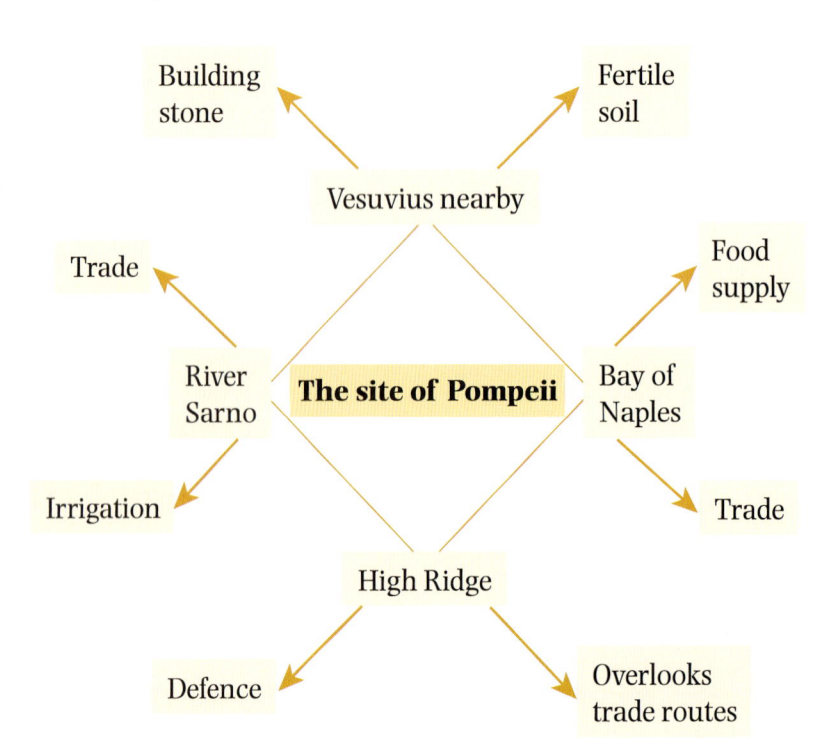

You have **four** key facts. You can now link each to **two** key consequences:

```
         Building              Fertile
          stone                 soil
            ↖                  ↗
              Vesuvius nearby

  Trade                                    Food
     ↖                                    supply
                                           ↗
        River      The site of    Bay of
        Sarno       Pompeii       Naples
       ↙                                    ↘
  Irrigation                                 Trade

              High Ridge
            ↙           ↘
       Defence         Overlooks
                       trade routes
```

In conclusion:

- There are many ways of organising knowledge so that it is not just in note form. The more you do this the more you will remember.
- The more you can remember, the more you will have at your fingertips to discuss.
- Added to this, the multiple choice questions in Part 1 will not be asking for obscure pieces of knowledge. They will be asking for key facts, the kind you will be identifying and highlighting in exercises such as the one above.

There is every reason for you to enjoy your study of the classical world. Following the simple advice above, working hard on the information in this book and identifying the key areas of fact, understanding and evaluation will enable you to achieve the best grade of which you are capable and one of which you can be proud.

SECTION TWO

CONTROLLED ASSESSMENT UNIT

2.1 Sophocles, Antigone

Creon has ordered on pain of death that Polyneices' body must not be buried. Antigone insists on burying it, and is proud of her action. The situation is made more tense by the fact that Antigone is engaged to Creon's son, Haemon. This is a play about a head of state putting power above morality; the dangers of being too proud and not listening to advice; conflicts within families and the destruction they cause – all things which concern us today as much as they did the ancient Greeks.

Characters

Antigone

Unlike her sister, Ismene, she challenges her uncle, and buries her brother. We focus on her in the first part of the play as she argues with her uncle, and eventually goes off to die, expressing her devotion to her tragic family and also her sorrow at dying unmarried.

Is she a courageous young woman who bravely defies her tyrannical uncle in order to do what she believes is morally right? Study what she says about her reasons for burying her brother. Is she consistent in her reasons?

Is she a girl obsessed with following her father to a tragic end, who has no-one but herself to blame for her situation? Find evidence to support the view that she is her own worst enemy. She had the opportunity to get away after the second burial when there was a sandstorm. Why did she cry out and draw attention to herself when she could have escaped?

A picture of Antigone visiting her brother's grave as imagined by a vase-painter. How does this image differ from the account in the play?

Creon

He stubbornly refuses to listen to advice, and insists on sending Antigone to her death. He changes his mind only when it is too late, and loses not only his niece, but his son and wife as well.

Is he a cruel tyrant, or a new leader doing his best to maintain stability? In what respects is he the opposite of Antigone? In what ways is he very like her? What is his attitude towards women?

Why might a 5th-century Athenian have had some sympathy for him? As well as ruler, he is husband, father and uncle. How do his actions destroy his family?

What is the final image in the play? How does it affect you? Do you feel more sympathy for Antigone or Creon at the end of the play?

Ismene

She is a contrast to Antigone, and allows her sister's character to be thrown in sharp relief.

Draw up a list of words and phrases that she uses to describe Antigone. Are her descriptions justified? What does she say about her own position?

Do you feel sympathy for her reaction to Creon's edict? Is she sensible or a coward?

Haemon

He is engaged to Antigone, but we never see them together: Sophocles does not want to focus on romantic love. We see him, instead, trying to persuade his father to change his mind.

What qualities does he show in the discussion with his father?

Examine the way Sophocles uses Haemon to help us understand other characters. He is young, but wise, compared with his father, who is old but acting foolishly. He emphasises Antigone's female side, reminding us that she is not just the rebellious daughter of Oedipus, but a young girl, whose tragedy is that she will never marry and have children.

The Sentry

His main function in the plot is that he discovers Antigone burying the body, and brings her to Creon. Sophocles uses him to great dramatic effect: his

Controlled Assessment Unit

delay in telling Creon creates tension; his fear reinforces the widespread effect of Creon's order; he has his own perspective on the burial, and his concern with self-preservation presents another moral question for the audience to ponder.

The role of women

Read page 14 about Athenian women, not because Antigone is a 5th-century Athenian woman, but so that you can appreciate better how a 5th-century Athenian male audience might have responded to the play. The play opens with two women outside the palace, a sure sign that something is wrong and that the male order has been disrupted. Women, as the Greek audience would have understood, belong inside.

After Antigone has announced her intention to bury her brother, Ismene gives her reasons for not joining in. What does she say about being a woman?

What regrets does Antigone express as she goes to her tomb?

How does Creon react at being defied by a woman? Find some quotations which reflect his feelings about women.

The chorus

The **stasima** (choral odes) were times when the chorus would dance together in choreographed movement, to the accompaniment of the double flute, or **auli**. Their language is highly poetic.

Study the **stasima**. Give each of them a title which reflects its content.

What do we hear in the **stasima** about:

- the achievements of man
- people who ignore justice
- the gods
- families which have been devastated by the gods
- the power of love
- mythological characters with resemblances to Antigone and Creon
- Dionysus and Thebes
- wisdom.

2.1 Sophocles, Antigone

Look at how the chorus interact with the characters throughout the play. Find examples of how they:

- introduce characters as they enter
- stress the power of the gods
- show sympathy for characters
- make remarks full of foreboding
- remind humans of their limitations
- comment on a character's actions to heighten the tension
- give advice
- act as umpire
- calm characters down
- express the views/doubts of the audience
- set the atmosphere.

The gods, oracles and fate

In Sophocles' world the gods are powerful. Humans must honour them with prayers and offerings, because to anger them will bring punishment. In Sophocles' play *Oedipus the King*, Oedipus' parents are told that their son will kill his father. Oedipus is told that he will kill his father and marry his mother. This goes on to happen, and Antigone is the daughter of Oedipus' union with his own mother.

In *Antigone* Tiresias, the prophet who never lies, arrives just after Antigone has been sent to be walled up, and warns Creon that the birds are killing each other, and offerings are refusing to burn on the altars – sure signs that the gods are angry. The prophet advises him to give up his pride and bury the body, but Creon mocks him, driving him to utter his terrible prophecy, that the avenging gods are lying in wait for him, and that he will have to pay for his crime with his own flesh and blood.

Find out more about Apollo's oracle at Delphi.

What does the chorus say about the power of the gods?

Find evidence to support the view that the gods' anger carries on from one generation to the next.

Is fate imposed from the outside, or do the characters bring about what happens through their own personalities and actions?

Controlled Assessment Unit

Sophocles' literary and dramatic techniques

Read pages 29–31 in order to familiarise yourself with the conventions of Greek tragedy. When you read the play, remember that *Antigone* was created to be performed with music and dancing. You'll need to use your imagination!

Sophocles introduces a third actor. This enables him to explore the burial of the body from many perspectives. For whom does the burial represent:

- an opportunity to show that the family is more important than the state
- a test of authority
- an opportunity for glory
- a threat to his job and life
- an example that the gods should be obeyed
- a choice between morality and common sense?

The minor characters represent a series of contrasts and balances, and the timing of their appearance in the play increases the tension.

To whom is Ismene a contrast, and in what way? Whom does she parallel in her role? Haemon enters the play halfway through. How does his appearance help to focus the interest on Creon himself? Why does Sophocles choose to show Eurydice briefly on stage?

Death and violence were not shown on stage. Sophocles uses a messenger to relate the deaths of Antigone, Haemon and Eurydice. Notice how vivid and dramatic the messenger's speech is.

Reversals and ironies run throughout the play:

- The son has wisdom, the father is foolish.
- The dead are unburied, the live are buried.
- Creon acts to establish his authority and ends up losing it; he claims to represent the state, but refuses to listen to the people's reactions to his decree. He forbids Antigone to satisfy the demands of her blood relationship with her family, and ends up destroying his own family. He accuses Antigone of having a stubborn will, but he is just as stubborn himself.
- The young girl who should be producing children is going to die without marrying.
- The father destroys his son.

2.1 Sophocles, Antigone

- The blind prophet sees the truth.
- When Creon realises that he should do what Tiresias said, he buries the body first, thus arriving too late to save Antigone.
- Man is all powerful, but cannot triumph over death.

Sophocles' language is rich in imagery. Look for examples of birds, animals, weather, light and dark, and marriage. What is the effect of this imagery?

The continuing influence of Antigone

The play raises the question of standing up to a tyrant and risking your life in the process, something which has universal relevance.

Both Jean Anouilh and Bertolt Brecht saw in *Antigone* a parallel to the aggression of the Nazis, with Antigone as the resistance, and wrote their own versions of the play. More recently, Seamus Heaney's version, called *The Burial at Thebes*, was prompted by the Iraq situation.

The play also owes its continuing relevance to the many themes which still fascinate us today. See if you can find newspaper headlines or television programmes which echo some of the following concerns as raised in *Antigone*:

- Rulers should listen to public opinion.
- Man should recognise his limitations.
- Women should know their place.
- Following your conscience is more important than obeying the law.
- Every dead person, even a traitor, has the right to a decent burial.
- Some people cause their own downfall through their own stubbornness.
- Some families seem prone to disasters.
- Can anyone foretell the future?

2.2 Aristophanes, Lysistrata

Think about the main argument of this play. The women are having a sex strike because they are fed up with their husbands being away at war all the while.

Now, if the men are not around, what difference can it make to them if their wives are on a sex strike? And even if they were around, it would be acceptable for them to turn to slaves or prostitutes if their wives rejected them. And how would women from different Greek states manage to travel and meet together in peacetime, let alone during a war? And why should the women think that their action could possibly influence a war? If you apply your cold logic to the play, then *Lysistrata* is hardly a success!

As you read it you must try to reconstruct in your mind the original performance – the audience on holiday and looking forward to good entertainment; Aristophanes wanting to win the competition and so constructing a play with the sort of outrageous humour that will get his work noticed. There is the laughter that is generated when 15,000 people watch a comedy together, and the brief escape from the suffering of war that the festival gives the Athenians. And remember, too, that it is likely that the audience was exclusively male.

If you look at *Lysistrata* as a 5th-century Athenian might have done, you will realise that the illogicalities would have not come into anyone's mind in the excitement of the first production in 411 BC.

The Characters

Lysistrata

When you study a character in a novel you are generally dealing with a psychological portrait which the author is expecting you to understand and dwell on as you read. You must be careful not to approach Lysistrata in the same way. In creating a woman who stood up to men publicly, hoped to influence a war, and used force to take over the Acropolis, Aristophanes is creating an unrealistic figure. Remember that the audience was probably all male.

Would 5th-century Athenian men, whose wives ideally stayed indoors and certainly had no involvement in politics, have taken Lysistrata seriously?

2.2 Aristophanes, Lysistrata

In many ways, she comes from the realms of fantasy, yet her name, which means 'dissolver of armies', resembles closely the name of a priestess of the goddess Athena, well known to Athenians of the time. She commands respect from the other women, who adopt her plan. Her argument is that men should approach the running of the city with the same approach that women have to the organisation of their wool-making. This is logical and indicates common sense.

Might the audience have been caused, by the presentation of her character, to realise that women *can* make sensible contributions?

Calonice

She is important at the beginning of the play, as a foil to Lysistrata and example of the stereotypical sex-mad woman as portrayed by Aristophanes.

Find examples of the innuendos in her words to Lysistrata.

Myrrhine and Cinesias

We see little of Myrrhine at the beginning, just sufficient to prepare us for the scene at the end when she taunts her desperate husband, Cinesias.

Go through the scene, noting all the opportunities for laughter. You will have to use your imagination for the visual humour!

Lampito

She appears only at the beginning, as she has to return to Sparta and enlist her fellow Spartan women in the sex strike. She provides humour for the audience, who no doubt enjoyed laughing at what they saw as the typical Spartan woman.

What particular qualities does she have?

Read pages 102–104 to find out about women in Sparta.

The Magistrate or Proboulos

He arrives at the Acropolis to get money from the Treasury to pay for some timber needed for oars, and this leads to a confrontation with the women. He and the policemen he has brought with him are easily overcome by Lysistrata and her companions.

Controlled Assessment Unit

What can you find out about the role of a Proboulos?

How does Aristophanes make him appear ridiculous?

The Spartan Ambassador and Athenian Negotiator

You might expect these characters to engage in meaningful political discussion. Their minds, however, are too preoccupied with their physical discomfort to think about anything other than sex!

How seriously would the audience take them?

The Chorus

There are two choruses: one of old men, one of women. Why does Aristophanes divide the chorus into two, do you think?

As the old men climb up to the Acropolis, carrying fire so that they can smoke the women out, they sing about battles with Sparta long ago. Look carefully at the picture they give of the Spartans. Given what had happened in the war against Sparta in the years just before the production of *Lysistrata*, how do you think the audience would have reacted to their words?

Stratyllis appears to be making a serious point about women's contribution to the state, but any seriousness is undermined as she beats the men's chorus leader with a shoe and bites him, whilst the women threaten to strike the men where it hurts most. In the arguments, who puts the stronger case?

Women

Read page 14 for an account of women in Athens. Do the women in *Lysistrata* resemble them at all?

Is this a play which criticises and mocks women? Was Aristophanes reinforcing the old jokes about stereotypical women?

Think about the traditional male jokes which are made about women today. Is Aristophanes making similar jokes? Look for evidence of ancient Greek women being very fond of drinking, wearing make-up and clothes designed to seduce

2.2 Aristophanes, Lysistrata

men, or being obsessed with getting lovers. Look at their initial reaction to Lysistrata's proposal. What object do they swear on? What does the Magistrate say about their unbridled nature?

On the other hand, was Aristophanes trying to change his audience's view of women? Does he portray them in a sympathetic light? Who appears more sensible, Lysistrata or the Proboulos (magistrate)? In the choral passages, who comes off best, the women or the men?

How convincing is Lysistrata's argument that the men should run the city following the model of the women's wool-making? What exactly do the women want? Do they want to take over ruling Athens? Do they see themselves as taking over the men's jobs?

A woman spinning. What light does this throw on the way women are portrayed in the *Lysistrata*?

The women would have been played by men. Would this have had an effect on the reactions of the audience?

Dramatic and literary techniques

Read pages 29–31 to remind yourself of the conventions of comedy, which determined certain dramatic techniques.

Go through the play, working out how just three actors could have played all the parts (apart from Lysistrata herself, who is on stage most of the time). What made the quick changes of character possible in the Greek theatre?

Does the fact that the 'women' were actually men dressed up as women make the play more humorous?

The comedy is part of a festival to Dionysus, the god of wine and fertility, and the plays were performed on the slopes of the Acropolis. In what ways do the god and the city have a central role in the play?

The phallus is part of the traditional costume. How does Aristophanes exploit its humour in *Lysistrata*?

If you can't see a production of *Lysistrata*, at least watch a television comedy you enjoy, and try to analyse what it is that makes you laugh. You will probably find that the humour is very similar to that used by Aristophanes.

Look in *Lysistrata* for examples of:

Visual humour

- Unusual physical features or funny walks and gestures
- Farcical chasing, falling and fighting
- Crude gestures or inappropriate costume
- Throwing water
- Choreographed movement.

Verbal humour

- The meanings of the names of characters
- Crude terms and sexual innuendoes
- Puns, verbal abuse and scatological or sexual remarks
- Repetition, insults and mockery
- Unusual accents.

Situation

- Fantasy, parody or burlesque
- Role reversal.

Character

- Fantastic creations
- The fool who makes the audience feel superior
- Characters who represent vices
- Stereotypes the audience can love or mock.

Satire

- Of public figures
- Of political scandals
- Of unpopular leaders.

2.2 Aristophanes, Lysistrata

Historical and political context

It is important to bear in mind that for the audience, war with Sparta was a very real thing. *Lysistrata* was produced in 411 BC. Conflict with Sparta had been going on for 20 years, and a year previously news had reached Athens of the disastrous loss of the Athenian expeditionary force in Sicily. There was no sign of any political settlement. You can imagine that the Athenians would have appreciated this fantasy ending – a bit of relief from the stress of the real situation.

You will need to use the notes in your translation for help with understanding the political references. Remember that to an ancient Athenian the references would have been immediately recognisable and funny. Political satire soon dates. Can you think of any politicians today who are mocked through cartoons or references to their habits or actions? Aristophanes' plays and some television political satire have much in common.

Do you think that this play could change the audience's attitude towards the war with Sparta?

Can a modern audience not familiar with Greek history appreciate the play?

Lysistrata's influence

Lysistrata has been particularly popular in this country in recent years. More liberal approaches to sex have allowed a play previously viewed as pornographic to be performed without the erect phalloi being too shocking. The twentieth century also saw the rise of the feminist movement, which was delighted to have a Classical role model. Lysistrata has been held up as symbol of woman's fight against male dominance and her name has been frequently used in the women's anti-war movement.

2.3 The Olympic Games

Just as the sun shines brighter than any other star, so shines Olympia, putting all other games into the shade. (Pindar, *Olympian* 1.1)

As the poet Pindar claims, the Olympic Games were the greatest sporting event in the ancient world, just as the modern Olympic Games are in our world. How did they come to be held? What happened at the games? What was the site like? This section will give you pointers to find out more.

> **TAKING IT FURTHER**
>
> The ancient Olympics was one of four great games in ancient Greece. Find out about the other three games: **Nemean, Isthmian, Pythian.** Why were all four collectively known either as the 'sacred' games or the 'crown' games?

Origins

There are two different approaches to thinking about the origins of the Olympic Games – archaeology and mythology. Below are some ideas about how to investigate each one:

- **Archaeology.** Where in Greece was Olympia? What was special about the location? Were there any important cities nearby? What evidence is there for the earliest worship of Zeus at the site? When and how was the site of Olympia rediscovered in the modern age?
- **Mythology.** Find out about the foundation myths of Olympia and the games: Zeus and the thunderbolt, Pelops and Hippodamia, Herakles and the Augean stables. What can we learn about Olympia and the games from these myths? Do you think that there was truth in any of them?

> **TAKING IT FURTHER**
>
> How long did the ancient games last for? Why did they come to an end?

2.3 The Olympic Games

Evidence

How do we know what we do about the ancient Olympics? Find out about the travel writer **Pausanias**. How important is his account of the site of Olympia?

Who was **Pindar** and what sort of poems did he write? What can we learn about the games from him?

Choose three works of **Greek art** (pottery, painting or sculpture) and explain what they can teach us about athletic events. Works of art to examine could include a Panathenaic amphora, Myron's statue of a discus thrower or the bronze sculpture of the Delphic charioteer.

The Site of Olympia

Research and draw your own plan of the holy sanctuary at Olympia, the **Altis**. Why was it given this name?

Find out about the **Temple of Zeus** – what was the significance of its artistic decoration (the pediments and metopes)? Who built the statue of Zeus inside? What do we know about this statue? What was distinct about the altar of Zeus outside the temple? How do you think that a Greek visitor to the site would have felt when he saw the temple for the first time?

Temple of Zeus, Olympia.

Research the significance of the other buildings in and around the Altis: the **Temples** of **Hera** and **Meter**, the **Treasuries**, the **Stoa** of **Echo**, the **Zanes**, the **Bouleuterion**, the **Prytaneion**, the **Pelopeion**, the **Philippeon** and the **Leonidaion**. How do they compare to the buildings at a modern Olympic village?

What do we know about the **stadium** at Olympia? How similar do you think it was to a modern sporting stadium?

Controlled Assessment Unit

> **TAKING IT FURTHER**
>
> How much do you think we can learn about the ancient games from the buildings at Olympia? What do these buildings tell us about the religious nature of the festival?

The athletic events

The number of events at the games grew as the years passed. Find out how many events there were in the early festivals. In what order were events added after that? Were there any events which were dropped from the programme over the course of the centuries?

The events themselves can be divided into four categories: **running**, **equestrian**, **combat** and **pentathlon**. For each event, you should think about how it differs from its modern equivalent (if it is still practised).

- **Running**: how many running events were there? Why was the **stadion** the most important event at the games? What were the rules about starting a race and turning at the end of the track? What happened to competitors who false started?
- **Equestrian**: what can we learn from Pausanias about the Hippodrome at Olympia? Why was horse racing more dangerous in ancient times? What can you find out about how horses were trained? Who was awarded the prize after the equestrian events? Find out about the Athenian politician Alcibiades' entry of chariots at the games – what did he hope to gain by doing this?
- **Combat**: what were the rules in the pankration, boxing and wrestling events? What were ancient boxing gloves designed to do? Why do you think spectators enjoyed these events so much? Why do you think that boxing was believed to be the most dangerous of the three?
- **Pentathlon**: how do you think the winner of the pentathlon was decided and what are the different theories on this matter? There are also different theories about the ancient long jump – what are they and which one do you think is most likely to be the correct one? How are the discus and javelin different from their modern equivalents? To what extent do you think that a pentathlete had to be an 'all-round' athlete?

2.3 The Olympic Games

> **TAKING IT FURTHER**
>
> Many of the athletic events probably had their origins in training for war. Which ones do you think this applies to and why?

The athletes

What can you find out about the training that athletes did for the games? Do we know anything about their diets? What were the possible rewards for a victorious athlete, both at the games and when they returned to their home city? How were athletes received if they lost? What happened to athletes who cheated?

Find out about the achievements of the following ancient athletes: **Milo of Kroton, Diagoras of Rhodes, Leonidas of Rhodes, Sostratos of Sicyon**.

> **TAKING IT FURTHER**
>
> Find out about the nudity of ancient competitors. How is the word 'gymnasium' linked to the practice of athletes competing naked?

The festival

Preparations: research the role of the city of Elis in looking after the site of Olympia and organising the festival. What were the terms of the **Sacred Truce** and how was it announced? Why did the athletes have to spend a month in Elis before the festival? What can you find out about the two-day **procession** from Elis to Olympia immediately before the festival?

The programme: the Olympic festival lasted for five days. Find out what happened on each day. In addition to the sporting events, find out about the following: the swearing-in ceremony, the **funeral rites for Pelops**, the **victory celebrations**, the great **sacrifice of 100 oxen**, the **prize-giving**. What can we learn about the games from each of these events? Are there any similar sorts of celebrations in the modern Olympics?

Controlled Assessment Unit

The judges: how many judges were there and how were they selected? What were their duties before and during the games? How do their roles compare to those of modern Olympic judges?

The spectators: where did most of the spectators stay during the festival? What do you think conditions were like for them? What evidence is there to back this up? Why do you think that so many spectators came to Olympia? What else might they have seen apart from the sporting events? How does the experience of ancient spectators compare to that of modern spectators at the Olympics?

Women: were any women allowed to watch the games? How were women punished if they were caught at the Olympics? Why do you think that Greek men were so keen to prevent women from coming to the games?

Research the stories of: **Kallipateira of Rhodes** and **Kyniska of Sparta**.

Ancient and modern

The first Olympic Games of the modern era were held in Athens in 1896. Find out about the role of Baron Pierre de Coubertin in bringing the Olympics back to life.

How have the modern games changed over the last century or so? Create a table outlining the main similarities and differences between the ancient and the modern games.

2.4 Virgil, The Aeneid

The *Aeneid* is a good adventure story with fearsome monsters, perilous journeys, bloody battles, great passions and a brave hero with a quest to follow. However, it is more than just a story. It was composed just after Augustus established himself as emperor, and you can see how the values portrayed and the references to Rome's future and a ruler who will bring peace to the world are all designed to glorify the new ruler.

Aeneas and his mission

Aeneas' mission is to reach Italy and start a new race. Virgil includes in the narrative references to how great Rome will be. Look particularly at:

- Book 1, where Jupiter explains about Rome to Venus.
- Book 6, where Aeneas' father shows him the future.
- Book 8, where there are scenes from Roman history on his shield.

What Roman qualities are praised? Who is represented as being the greatest ever leader of Rome?

What feelings might these passages have inspired in Virgil's contemporaries?

The character of Aeneas

The character of Aeneas is very much bound up with his mission. He is the ideal Roman who embodies piety – the act of behaving correctly towards the gods, your country and your family.

Make a list of Aeneas' pious actions. Can you see why Augustus would like his citizens to behave in a similar way?

Do you admire Aeneas' behaviour in Book 4? His piety is praiseworthy, but isn't there something cowardly in the way he sneaks off without saying goodbye? (When Mark Antony, Augustus' great rival, was faced with another passionate queen in North Africa, he showed less loyalty and strength of character and abandoned his Roman wife to stay with Cleopatra.)

At many points in the story, Aeneas suffers as he pursues his mission. Notice his sadness when the dead Creusa appears, his shock when Mercury reminds

Controlled Assessment Unit

him he should not be in Carthage, and his pathetic attempts to grasp his father's ghost.

He is sometimes very hurt and angry. Look at how he reacts at the death of Pallas in Book 10. What do you think of his behaviour in the very last lines of the poem? Should he have listened when Turnus begged for his life? Would you describe his behaviour as heroic? To avenge the death of Pallas is honourable and heroic, but should he not have spared Turnus for his father's sake?

The role of the hero

Virgil modelled his epic on the *Iliad* and *Odyssey* of Homer, with their heroes Achilles and Odysseus. Achilles was concerned above all with his reputation and achieving glory for himself. He was brave, spontaneous, and a great warrior. Odysseus too was concerned with his reputation and renowned for his cunning and ingenuity. He remained confident throughout of his superior intelligence and place as rightful ruler of Ithaca.

Virgil, however, wanted to create a hero for the age of Augustus, one who could inspire the citizens of the early Empire who had recently seen their country torn apart by civil war.

Look for evidence of how Aeneas differs from these Homeric heroes. Is he concerned just for himself? Does he want glory? Is he sure of his destination? Does he have self-doubts? Is he spontaneous? Does he really want to be fighting in Italy?

Other characters

Dido

She is a noble and honourable queen, but a victim of the gods. Notice how she fights her passion, desperately tries to make Aeneas stay and then, once he has left, she gives herself over to thoughts of vengeance and death.

Examine all her speeches in detail, and trace how her feelings develop. Notice how emotional she is, while Aeneas remains calm.

At the end of Book 4, are your sympathies with Aeneas or Dido?

2.4 Virgil, The Aeneid

Turnus

He is the enemy of Aeneas, and the second half of the *Aeneid* is given over to their fighting. Look at the imagery used about him which paints him as a wild animal ready to attack.

Is he justified in opposing Aeneas? What heroic qualities does he have? What does he have in common with Dido? What does Virgil do to make you feel sympathy for him? Are you pleased when he is killed at the end?

Latinus and Amata

Latinus and Amata have different attitudes towards the arrival of Aeneas.

What difficulty does Latinus find himself in? What makes Amata so hostile to Aeneas?

Evander and Pallas

As father and son, they echo the great bond which Aeneas feels for Anchises and Ascanius. The killing of Pallas by Turnus is a crucial event for Aeneas. He feels terribly guilty that he has failed to protect Evander's son, and we see his raging anger as he is determined to get revenge.

Read the story of Lausus and Mezentius in Book 10 for another father and son story.

Juturna

She is a divine nymph who has the support of Juno. She can do supernatural things like change herself into Turnus' chariot driver and help him in the battle. Yet she is very human too: she is a sister who is desperately trying to save her brother's life. Her plight is even worse than her brother's in one respect: since she is immortal she can find no relief from her suffering in death.

The gods and fate

The involvement of the gods makes the poem interesting because there are, as it were, two layers of action – divine and human. Jupiter represents fate – what he says must happen, will happen.

Controlled Assessment Unit

Look at how the gods interfere with the action in order to support their favourites. Why does Juno not want Aeneas to reach Rome? What does Venus do to help Aeneas?

The beginning of Book 10 shows the Olympian family arguing about Aeneas' fate. Examine Juno and Venus' arguments to try to get Jupiter's support.

Why might Augustus have encouraged the depiction of an all-knowing, all-powerful god?

The actions of the gods mean that Aeneas is not in control. Does that alter your attitude towards him?

Virgil's literary technique

Look for:

Flashbacks (stories within stories): This narrative technique is typical of epic. Books 2 and 3 are a flashback as Aeneas tells Dido about his adventures. In Book 3 there is a digression as Polydorus relates his story, and the story of the Minotaur is introduced through the description of Daedalus' golden temple in Book 6. Look for other examples of stories being interwoven in the main narrative.

Speeches: Drama is added to the narrative by the use of direct speech. Find examples of speeches which heighten the emotional impact of the story.

Scenes of pathos: Aeneas undergoes great personal suffering as he is forced to leave his beloved Troy and pursue a mission which brings even more sadness. Study the language and images that Virgil uses to convey that suffering. There is an element of pathos in many of Virgil's characters. Dido is the outstanding example, but look too at Aeneas' enemies such as Turnus, whose vulnerability is emphasised, and Mezentius, who, although evil, is touched by the terrible sight of his son's sacrifice for his father. Even the Cyclops, Polyphemus, is presented as pathetic, and non-living beings suffer, such as the souls in Book 6.

Similes: Virgil's similes give a complete picture which can be interpreted on many levels. Consider the comparison of Dido to a deer in Book 4. Why does Virgil choose a deer? Why is it described as being off its guard? How does the image tell you about Dido's mental as well as physical state? Who is the hunter? Is he to blame? Why is he portrayed as being a long way away? What is the significance of the arrow? Will the deer die immediately? Is there any possibility that it will survive? Why is its fleeing futile? Chose other similes and ask yourself similar questions in order to tease out all the implications of the image.

Description: Virgil's description is so vivid, you could do a film storyboard for the scene of the sea monsters and Laocoon in Book 2. Find other examples of graphic description which has a cinematic quality. Look at how he conjures up atmosphere. How does he create the horror of the underworld in Book 6? What makes the cave in Book 4 so eerie? How is the panic evoked in the palace in Book 2?

Imagery: As you read, be aware of the images which reoccur, such as fire, wounds, arrows, animals, wild weather, strong trees, bristling corn and outstretched arms. How do the images give the story extra interest? Abstract powers given a physical form are another way Virgil makes the story more exciting, and at the same time shows how powerful certain emotions are. Look, for example at Rumour in Book 4, Allecto as the personification of burning jealousy and treachery in Book 7, and fear represented by Jupiter's demons in book 12.

Historical context

Virgil was born in 70 BC and for the first forty years of his life was familiar with the destruction of civil war. We see in the *Aeneid* how vividly he describes death and suffering, and how much he appreciates the peaceful countryside. It must have been a great relief for him when Octavian beat Antony at the battle of Actium in 31 BC, and finally there was peace in Rome under the stable rule of one man. Augustus (as Octavian now called himself) wanted Rome to return to its former greatness, and encouraged the values that had made it great: the old traditions, strong family affection, a sense of duty, respect for religion, loyalty and patriotism. Virgil started to write the *Aeneid* in 30 BC, and as we read it we can see how he too was promoting the same values through his story of Aeneas' journey to Italy.

Read about the civil wars and the eventual victory of Octavian over Mark Antony. Look at Augustus' use of propaganda to strengthen his power: his rebuilding of temples and revival of religious practices and his legal reforms to encourage more marriage and children. He projected his image through art and architecture and put great emphasis on traditional Roman values.

Useful primary sources include: Suetonius' *The Twelve Caesars*; the *Res Gestae* by Augustus himself; the Forum of Augustus in Rome; images in art, such as the Ara Pacis.

Controlled Assessment Unit

Aeneas makes a sacrifice in this scene from the Ara Pacis, an altar dedicated by the Emperor Augustus in 9 BC. As the *Aeneid* glorified Augustus and Rome in poetry, this altar to Peace used art to associate him with the glory of Rome's past.

Why is the *Aeneid* still popular and relevant?

The sheer number of translations, operas, paintings and sculptures based on the *Aeneid* throughout the centuries is evidence of how popular it has been since Virgil's time. Search for examples of them on the internet.

Using literature as part of a huge public relations campaign to win popularity for a new leader is a concept we are familiar with. How do leaders today use the arts to promote themselves?

What makes the *Aeneid* so influential?

- There is a hero on a quest, a long journey and the fight between good and evil. There is a lost father and loving son relationship. There is a destiny, there are monsters to overcome and the death of loved ones. Do you know any modern films and novels that use the same elements?
- Meeting fantastic monsters is exciting. Can you think of any late 20th-century three-headed guard dogs?
- Do people have free will or is your fate already decided? The number of people who read horoscopes is an indication that this question is still very much alive.

2.5 Pliny, Letters

Note: 1, 6 means Book 1, letter 6 etc.

As a successful lawyer, politician and writer, Pliny was a well-known figure in Rome. He began his career speaking in the law-courts in about 80 AD when he was only eighteen, and died in Bithynia in 113.

Research the **cursus honorum**, the career structure for a Roman politician.

Pliny wrote hundreds of letters. The letters mentioned below have been chosen for this chapter because they are relevant to the themes you are studying and will provide evidence that you may want to use in your essay. You are free, of course, to use any of Pliny's letters, not just the ones below. You will need to read the individual letters in detail and then select quotations which best support your argument.

Pliny's purpose in writing and publishing the letters

Pliny tells us in 1, 1 that Septicus Clarus has been urging him to publish his letters, and that he has finally collected them together. It was not an unusual thing to do: Cicero, the politician and lawyer, published his personal letters, and the poets Horace and Martial wrote verse letters for publication. Pliny composed his legal speeches with great care, and it is not surprising that he took similar care in the composition of his letters. It was natural for him to want to display his literary skills by showing off his compositions to a wider public.

Roman writing equipment, including a pair of wooden writing tablets, three pens to inscribe in wax and an ink pot.

Controlled Assessment Unit

Being remembered after your death was important to Romans, and certainly Pliny is concerned with his reputation and what future generations will think of him. Many of the letters talk about his care for friends and family, his generosity as a patron, and the love he inspires in those around him.

Many of the letters, though addressed to individuals, make moral, social or political points which Pliny wants to share. Through publishing his letters, he could condemn the behaviour of rogues, praise heroic individuals, or discuss principles of law.

In preparing letters for publication, is it possible that Pliny would have made a few changes to the original versions? Why might it be tempting to do so?

What sort of people would want to read his letters? Would they be typical Romans?

How do present-day people like Pliny publicise their views?

What problems would Pliny have had with writing about politics when Domitian was emperor? Read about Domitian in *The Twelve Caesars* by Suetonius to find out what sort of man this emperor was.

Pliny's character

We can tell much about Pliny's character from the subject matter of his letters.

He loves literature

- 1, 6 he takes his writing materials with him, even when he goes hunting;
- 1, 9 he loves going to his country houses, where he can spend all his time reading and writing;
- 1, 13 he expresses his delight that so many poets are writing and reciting their work;
- 7, 20 he is a close friend of Tacitus, the historian, and they comment on each other's work.

What sort of education did the average Roman receive? How typical do you think Pliny's behaviour is?

He is sociable and values his friends

- 1, 15 he writes to a friend who did not turn up to a dinner party;
- 1, 19 he gives an old friend a large sum of money so that he can become a knight;
- 5, 2 he sends a thank you letter to the sender of some fine thrushes (to eat).

If you look at the houses and wall-paintings in Pompeii you will see that dinner parties were a very important part of a rich Roman's lifestyle. Where did the poor eat, though, and what was their diet like?

He likes being busy

- 3, 1 he describes how 78-year-old Spurinna spends his days as a good example of keeping active;
- 3, 5 he writes in praise of his uncle, who never wasted a moment;
- 9, 36 his routine in the country.

Did all Romans use their time so well? Read Juvenal *Satires* 1 or look at the evidence in Pompeii for some less healthy activities!

He hates crowds and non-intellectual pursuits

9, 6 he hates being in Rome when the chariot racing is on. He considers it a useless occupation and cannot see its appeal.

Research the Colosseum and Circus Maximus in Rome. Were most Romans like Pliny?

He is a generous patron

- 4, 1 he has built a temple for the people of Tifernum-on-Tiber and is going to the dedication ceremony;
- 4, 13 he is helping to set up a school in his home town of Comum.

Why was he so generous, do you think? Do rich people do similar things today?

He hates vulgar people

- 2, 6 he is shocked by a man who ranks his friends at his dinner parties;
- 4, 2 he is critical of Regulus, who is mourning his son in an extravagant way.

Controlled Assessment Unit

The Satires of Juvenal and Horace, and Petronius' *Trimalchio's Dinner Party* give some wonderful examples of vulgar people. What do we consider vulgar today?

He loves his country houses

- 2, 8 he longs to be reading, fishing or hunting in the country;
- 2, 17 he describes in detail his villa at Laurentum;
- 5, 6 he describes his villa in Tuscany;
- 9, 36 he describes his summer days in Tuscany.

Research the living conditions in an **insula**, or look at Juvenal's description of one in *Satires* 3. How typical was Pliny's lifestyle?

How typical of Roman life is the picture we get from the letters? Read what Pliny's contemporaries such as Juvenal or Martial have to say.

Pliny's relationship with his household

A Roman household was much larger than a present-day household. It was made up of the parents and children, but also other relatives who lived in the house, such as grandparents, and slaves and freedmen (see pages 32–35).

His wife

In his letters Pliny writes of devoted wives, long marriages, and couples who share their troubles. He clearly has hopes of a long and happy marriage with Calpurnia, his third wife. She was about 15, he over 40, but the age difference was acceptable and not unusual in a time when marriage was for producing an heir. His attitude towards her seems almost paternal at times, as he praises the way she admires his writing, for example, but he clearly loves her and misses her when she is away.

- 4, 19 Pliny writes to his wife's aunt to say what a wonderful wife Calpurnia is;
- 6, 4 Calpurnia is in Campania and he is missing her;
- 6, 7 the only comfort Pliny gets when Calpurnia is away is from reading her letters;
- 7, 5 he is in misery because Calpurnia is not there;
- 8, 10 he writes to Calpurnia's grandfather to say that she has had a miscarriage;
- 8, 11 he writes to her aunt to say that she has recovered.

2.5 Pliny, Letters

This, of course, is Pliny's side of the story. How might a 15-year-old girl feel about being married to a very serious, intellectual and well-regarded 40-year-old?

His wife's grandfather

Calpurnia's grandfather, Calpurnius Fabatus, did not live in the household, but is an important figure for Pliny.

- 4, 1 Pliny is looking forward to visiting him with his wife;
- 5, 11 Calpurnius Fabatus has just dedicated a colonnade in his own name and that of his son. Pliny is pleased that this will enhance the family's reputation;
- 6, 30 he sends birthday wishes and discusses home maintenance;
- 6, 12 he replies to criticism.

His uncle

His uncle, known as Pliny the Elder, was a great influence in Pliny's life, and the letters about him stress his heroism when Vesuvius erupted, and his devotion to hard work throughout his life.

- 3, 5 Pliny provides a biography of his uncle;
- 6, 16 he describes his uncle's death in the eruption of Vesuvius.

Is his uncle heroic or foolish in sailing towards Pompeii? Should he really be praised for his refusal to waste time, or is he abnormally obsessed?

Families are important in Roman society. Look at the household shrines and busts of the ancestors found in Pompeii. What difference does your family status make if you want to be a politician?

Slaves

Slaves were an accepted part of Roman life, and even the most humane and educated of men, such as Pliny, did not question their existence. Pliny seems to have an underlying fear of what slaves are capable of as he recounts the murder of a master, yet he shows himself to be kind to the slaves in his household.

- 3, 14 he writes about the shocking murder of Larcius Macedo by his own slaves, and points out how all masters ought to be wary of their slaves;
- 5, 19 he shows concern for his freedman, Zosimus, who is ill;
- 8, 16 he explains how well he treats his slaves.

Controlled Assessment Unit

How consistent is Pliny in his views about slaves? Does he express the same opinion about them in all his letters?

Pliny's role as provincial governor

In 109 or 110 AD Pliny was sent as the special envoy of the Emperor Trajan to the province of Bithynia. Public money was being wasted on building projects, there was political disorder, and there were irregularities in administration. Pliny had considerable experience in financial management, and Trajan sent him to Bithynia to put things right.

How had Pliny's career prepared him for this job?

Trajan had encouraged Pliny to consult him if he had queries. Here are some of Pliny's questions (and Trajan's answers):

- 10, 19 and 20 'Should public slaves or soldiers be used as prison warders?'
- 10, 31 and 32 'Should convicts be allowed to work as public slaves?'
- 10, 33 and 34 'May I form a fire brigade?'
- 10, 37 and 38 'Can I have an architect or engineer to finish an aqueduct in Nicomedia?'
- 10, 39 and 40 'Can you please send an architect to look at the theatre and gymnasium at Nicaea, and the baths at Claudiopolis?'
- 10, 43 and 44 'Do you approve of my cutting travel expenses for a delegation of officials?
- 10, 96 and 97 'What shall I do with the Christians?'
- 10, 98 and 99 'May I cover a sewer in Amastris?'
- 10, 120-121 'I gave my wife a permit to use the imperial post. Do you mind?'

A few letters are on a personal level. For example: 10, 15–17 Pliny announces his arrival in Bithynia.

- Is Pliny genuinely friendly with Trajan, or is he being the subservient employee?
- Does Pliny lack confidence?
- Does Trajan feel real affection for Pliny, or is he just being polite?
- Does he trust Pliny? Does he welcome all Pliny's questions?

2.6 Roman Britain

To the Romans, Britain lay on the edge of the world. Indeed, they believed that the island lay in the Ocean which encircled the lands of the earth. Britain was therefore seen as distant, dangerous and mysterious. Conquering this island would show that the Romans were truly masters of the world.

Pre-Roman Britain

To understand Roman Britain properly, it is important to find out what we can about the peoples who lived in Britain before the Roman invasion. However, this is no easy task. Our first written sources on Britain are Roman ones, and so we have to rely on archaeology to reconstruct what life must have been like in iron-age Britain. To find out about this period, you could concentrate on the following themes:

- **Trade.** What evidence is there for trade between the peoples of Britain and continental Europe? When was coinage introduced to Britain?
- **Tribes.** How many tribal groupings are there thought to have been in Britain? Find out what you can about the **Regnenses**, the **Iceni**, the **Brigantes**, the **Catuvellauni** and the **Deceangli**.
- **Hill forts.** Find out about hill forts such as Maiden Castle and Hod Hill. How were they used and how important were they for the surrounding people?

> **TAKING IT FURTHER**
>
> There are two early Roman accounts of what the ancient Britons looked like. Read the words of Caesar, *Gallic War* V.12–14 and the geographer Strabo in his *Geography* IV.5.2. What do we learn here? How accurate do you think these accounts are likely to be?

Evidence

How do we know what we do about Roman Britain? Various Roman writers have left us with interesting (if subjective) accounts. Find out about the following writers and what they tell us about Roman Britain: **Julius Caesar, Strabo, Suetonius, Tacitus** and **Dio Cassius.**

The other main source of evidence is from archaeology, and in studying Roman Britain you will need to research sites such as Bath, Chester and Hadrian's Wall. Where is the nearest Roman British site to where you live? What can you find out about the influence of Roman Britain in your area?

The invasions

Julius Caesar: The Romans did not conquer Britain until 43 AD. However, nearly a century before this, Julius Caesar launched two speculative invasions in successive years: 55 and 54 BC. Read Caesar's account of these two invasions (*Gallic War* IV.20–38 and V.1–23). Why do you think he wanted to invade Britain? How successful was he on each occasion?

Claudius: A full-scale invasion was then launched by the emperor Claudius in 43 AD. Read the accounts of Dio Cassius (LX.19–24) and Suetonius (*Claudius* 17). Why do you think that Claudius wanted to invade Britain? What alliances did he make with local British tribal chiefs? Find out about the expansion of the Romans into other parts of the island by reading Suetonius (*Vespasian* 4) and Tacitus (*Annals* X11.31–39).

Rebellions

There were two famous Roman British chiefs who resisted the advance of the Romans in Britain: Boudicca and Caratacus.

Boudicca was the husband of Prasutagus, the king of the Iceni, a people who were clients and allies of the Romans. However, when Prasutagus died, a dispute over his will led to a terrible conflict. The key historical passages relating to the rebellion are by Tacitus (*Annals* XIV.29–37) and Dio Cassius (LXII.1–12). Use these texts to research the following aspects of the revolt:

- What were the causes of the rebellion? How were Boudicca and her daughters treated by the Romans after her husband's death? What grievances did the Trinovantes have which caused them to join the fight?

2.6 Roman Britain

- How successful was the revolt? What happened in Colchester, London and St Albans? What was the fate of the ninth Hispanic Legion? How did the Romans win the final battle and what do we know about the fate of Boudicca?

Caratacus was the son of Cunobelinus, king of the Catuvellauni. He is believed to have led much of the resistance to the Roman invasion. Read Tacitus' account of his resistance (*Annals* XII.31–38). How objective do you think Tacitus' account can have been, and what reasons might he have had to exaggerate the bravery and nobility of Caratacus?

Romanisation

As the Romans gained control over most of Britain, they introduced a policy of 'Romanisation' – the idea that native Britains could be made to accept and appreciate Roman culture. At the head of this policy was **Gnaeus Julius Agricola**, the governor of the province between 78 and 85 AD. Agricola is the subject of a biography by Tacitus (who just happened to be his son-in-law!) and this is essential reading for students of Roman Britain. In *Agricola* 21, Tacitus explains how the governor introduced Romanising measures, encouraging communities to build towns on the Roman model and educating the sons of the native nobility in the Roman manner.

The Roman town. The Romans were keen to build towns so that native peoples could benefit from Roman civilisation – by enjoying the baths, the theatre and the amphitheatre, as well as appreciating the prosperity brought by large markets. Research a town of Roman Britain of your choice; find out about its **grid layout, forum** and **basilica**. What other notable features did it have? What was the difference between a **colonia** and a **municipium**?

Perhaps the most famous example of Romanisation is the town of Bath – known to the Romans as **Aquae Sulis**. This provides vital evidence for life in Roman Britain and should be a key part of your study of Roman Britain. You could research the following topics:

- What evidence is there for religion at the site of the baths? Who was the goddess **Sulis Minerva**? What does this goddess say about Roman tolerance for local religion? What were 'curse tablets' and what can we learn about local beliefs from them?

Controlled Assessment Unit

- What can we learn about the people who worked at and used the baths? What types of archaeological evidence survive for us to study?

The Roman villa. You might also examine how the Romans operated in the countryside. A villa could either be a large farming estate or a lavish country house for a wealthy Romano-British family. Choose a Roman villa in Britain which has been extensively excavated today – you might look at Chedworth or Lullingstone. What evidence is there for the functions of these estates and their relationship to the local community? What can we learn about the people who lived there?

The Great Bath at Bath.

Chester: a Roman fortress town

A key element of life in the provinces of Roman Britain was the presence of the Roman army. Some towns were built by the Romans to be permanent bases for their legions; the most famous of these was Chester (known as **Deva** in Roman times).

> ### TAKING IT FURTHER
>
> Today there are many towns and cities in Britain whose names end in the suffix **-chester** or **-cester**. This comes from the Latin **castra**, meaning camp, and indicates that the place originally had a large Roman encampment there. How many place names with this suffix can you think of?

Chester was home to a fortress, a permanent home to a Roman legion. It was built with barracks, granaries, military headquarters (**principia**), legionary baths, and an unusual round building that may have acted

168

2.6 Roman Britain

as the governor of Britain's headquarters. Research the following topics relating to Chester:

- What was the geographical importance of the city in Roman Britain?
- Find out about the layout and defences of the fortress as an example of a typical Roman military base.
- How did the development of the fortress allow a town to grow up around it? Find out what you can about the civilian settlement and the impact of the occupation on the local area.
- What can we learn about the organisation of the Roman army and a soldier's life from the evidence at Chester?

Hadrian's Wall

Hadrian's Wall is the most famous symbol of Roman Britain. Learning about it tells us much about life on the frontier of the Roman Empire and relations with other peoples. In your research, find out the following:

- The length and dimensions of the wall, and how it was built.
- Why the wall was built and what purpose it served.
- The military road, milecastles, turrets and forts along the wall – you may wish to concentrate on one fort such as Housesteads.
- What evidence there is for the military, social and religious life of soldiers living on the wall. In particular, find out about the **Vindolanda tablets** and what they tell us about the people who lived on the wall.
- What can we learn about the organisation of the Roman army on the wall.

> **TAKING IT FURTHER**
>
> What do you think is the legacy of Roman Britain in modern Britain today? What similarities and differences can you find between Britain under the Romans and Britain today? Would Britain be a very different country if the Romans had not colonised it for 400 years?

2.7 Preparing for the controlled assessment

In the other units you have to learn all the information thoroughly and then be prepared to answer examination questions which test facts and your understanding of them. This unit, Culture and Society in the Classical World (the controlled assessment), is different. The topics are similar – some are historical and some based on literature – but the emphasis here is on your ability to look at the **primary evidence**, and draw your own conclusions.

The controlled assessment is an essay of 2000 words which you research in advance and write in class under supervision at the end of your course.

Your teacher will introduce a topic from those on offer. You will be given a title to work on, and advice on where you can research evidence (the school library, the internet, sourcebooks, archaeological sites and reports etc). It will be your job to select the evidence which will be most effective in answering the essay question.

Organisation

You will have to be well organised:

- Make sure you have a schedule. Don't leave your research until the last minute.
- If you are storing your research on computer, make sure you have a back-up.
- Keep your paper research in a file under appropriate headings. Don't let vital bits of evidence get crumpled at the bottom of your school-bag!
- Be very strict about keeping records of the source of your research. If you use material without saying where you got it from, you could find yourself being accused of plagiarism (copying other people's work).
- Bear in mind that your essay has to be only 2000 words long. At some point you will find that the best thing is to stop researching and start thinking more carefully about how you can *use* the material you have. Your teacher will be able to advise you when you have done enough research.
- When you go over your research, remember that your evidence has to be chosen to suit the essay question. Make sure you know what the focus of

2.7 Preparing for the controlled assessment

the discussion will be. Don't be tempted to include material just because it is interesting. It must be relevant to your title.
- Make sure well in advance that you know how much relevant factual material you intend to include.
- With the teacher's help and advice make sure you have an amount that you can incorporate into your work in the time limit of the supervised session or sessions.

You can take your research materials into the controlled assessment, but you can't draft the essay in advance. You have to write that from scratch while being supervised.

Marking the controlled assessment

Your teacher will mark your work according to detailed instructions. You will be able to increase your chances of a high mark if you know what the teacher is going to be awarding marks for.

There are three headings under which marks are awarded. These are the same areas which are tested in the written examination, but the controlled assessment takes a slightly different approach to them. This is what you have to do to get **top marks** under each heading.

Knowledge (21 marks)
- You show thorough knowledge of the subject in the title.
- You show off your knowledge by presenting factual information and a range of evidence from primary sources.
- Spelling, punctuation and grammar are accurate, and your meaning is clear.
- Your essay should be within the 2000 word limit.

Understanding (18 marks)
- You show a thorough understanding of the issues raised by the title, and explain them clearly.
- You show you understand the values of the society in which the evidence was produced.
- You show a thorough understanding of the evidence, with clear and detailed explanation of why it is relevant and contributes to your work.

Controlled Assessment Unit

Interpretation and evaluation (21 marks)
- You show a thorough evaluation of the issues raised by the title.
- You use primary sources effectively as evidence for your opinions.
- You draw sensible conclusions from the facts and evidence that you include.
- You explain clearly and logically why you reached these conclusions.
- You show that you have thought for yourself about the answer.

In marking your work the teacher will not be looking for a specific answer. You may approach the question from a slightly different angle to your classmates and come up with a different conclusion – that's fine! What counts is what you include in your work, how you discuss it and whether you provide a convincing case, with evidence, to justify your opinions.

Interpreting evidence

Primary evidence, or **source material** as it is sometimes called, is things that were written, built or created by the ancient Greeks or Romans themselves. It includes plays, poems, letters, inscriptions, bones, artefacts such as pottery or jewellery and buildings. The idea is that you examine the evidence, and using your background information about the society to help you, you draw conclusions.

However, before you draw conclusions, you need to think carefully about how you **interpret** primary evidence. This means asking yourself questions as you look at your source material.

If you are looking at a **building** or an **artefact**, ask yourself:

- Which geographical area does the find come from?
- Is a find from that area relevant to what I am investigating?
- What date is it?
- Is the date relevant to the time I am investigating?
- Does this evidence apply to all social classes?
- Does it apply to both men and women?
- Is the identification certain or do archaeologists argue about what it is?

For example, Romano-British villas were often modified over the years. Make sure that you are not using 4th-century remains for an investigation about the 2nd century!

2.7 Preparing for the controlled assessment

If you are studying **art**:

- Is this sculpture or drawing meant to be factually correct?
- Is it produced for a particular purpose?
- Is it in its original setting?

For example, does a mosaic of Venus in a Romano-British villa tell you that the inhabitants worshipped Venus or that they admired Roman culture, or that they had it for decoration without really thinking about what it represented?

Don't accept **written evidence** at face value. Ask yourself:

- Why has the author written this? Is it to entertain? Is it to criticise?
- Is it likely to be biased?
- Is the writer typical of his period?
- Is there more than one interpretation?

For example, why do Pliny's letters all show him in a very favourable light? Did Athenian women really behave like those in Lysistrata?

You must always balance what the evidence *does* tell you with what it *doesn't* tell you.

Imagine, what would an archaeologist living two thousand years in the future conclude about life in Britain today on the basis of the sort of random finds that archaeologists studying the classical world have to deal with?

- **Find**: the remains of a steam engine. **Conclusion**: this was the way people travelled in the 20th-century.
- **Find**: a picture of a Hallowe'en party. **Conclusion**: people believed that witches with black cats flew around on broomsticks.
- **Find**: the scripts for *Fawlty Towers* or *Scrubs*. **Conclusion**: this is what all hotels or hospitals were like!

When you examine your Greek or Roman evidence, you must make sure that you don't leap to such simple conclusions!

Writing your essay

When you write your essay, you will have to use your primary source material as a basis for your argument. Here are some tips:

Controlled Assessment Unit

Don't assume that people in the ancient world thought exactly as we do nowadays.

Here are some examples of differences in the way of thinking:

- Even civilised and humane people accepted slavery.
- The main role of women was to produce children. They didn't have careers.
- Religion was not concerned with giving people instructions about how to live their lives.

Living conditions were very different:

- Life expectancy was very short.
- There was no printing, and so books were rare.
- All entertainment was live.
- Travel was difficult and dangerous.

So remember that you must not interpret words said 2000 years ago as if they were written in modern times. Don't, for example, blame Pliny's young wife for not behaving like a girl alive today, or see Lysistrata as a 20th-century suffragette!

And finally, use your evidence effectively when you are doing your essay:

- If you are writing about literature, keep your quotations short. Select only the words which are necessary to support your point.
- If you are using pictures, don't treat them as decoration. They must be there as part of your argument. Annotate them to let your reader know why they are good evidence.

The chapters in section 2 of this book will give you an outline of the topics which can be researched and how to approach them, but the controlled assessment is really a piece of work that relies on your own commitment. Get ahead and don't leave things too late.

Further Reading

Websites

www.ancientgreece.co.uk Includes a wide range of resources from the British Museum.

www.bbc.co.uk/history/ancient

www.classicspage.com News, information, games and controversy.

http://www.fordham.edu/halsall/ancient/asbook07.html The 'Internet Ancient History Sourcebook' – provides original source material.

www.insearchofthegreeks.com Many of the best websites are linked from this site.

http://www.omnibusol.com/angreece.html An enormous range of links for Greece.

http://www.omnibusol.com/anrome.html An enormous range of links for Rome.

www.perseus.tufts.edu Perseus digital library.

www.vroma.org A virtual community for teaching and learning classics.

Books

Colin Amery and Brian Curran, *The Lost World of Pompeii*, Getty

R. Barrow, *Greek and Roman Education* (Inside the Ancient World series), Bristol Classical Press

Peter Connolly and Hazel Dodge, *The Ancient City: Life in Classical Athens and Rome*, OUP

Peter Connolly, *Pompeii*, OUP

Matthew Dillon, *The Ancient Greeks in Their Own Words*, Sutton Publishing

J. Gibbon, *Athenian Society* (Inside the Ancient World series), Bristol Classical Press

Further Reading

S. Hill and S. Ireland, *Roman Britain* (Classical World series), Bristol Classical Press

Michael Massey, *Women in Ancient Greece and Rome*, CUP

Pliny, *A Selection of his Letters*, translated by Clarence Greig, CUP

James Renshaw, *In Search of the Greeks*, Bristol Classical Press

James Renshaw, *In Search of the Romans*, Bristol Classical Press (due 2010)

N. Sekunda, *The Spartans*, Osprey Military

Judith Swaddling, *The Ancient Olympic Games*, British Museum Press

Waldo Sweet, *Sport and Recreation in Ancient Greece*, OUP

D. Taylor, *Greek and Roman Stage* (Inside the Ancient World series), Bristol Classical Press

D. Taylor, *Roman Society* (Inside the Ancient World series), Bristol Classical Press

M. Thorpe, *Homer* (Inside the Ancient World series), Bristol Classical Press

Paul Wilkinson, *Pompeii: The Last Day*, BBC Books

Paul Wilkinson, *What the Romans Did for Us*, BBC Books

R. Williams, *Aeneas and the Roman Hero* (Inside the Ancient World series), Bristol Classical Press